Southern Living®

Wedding

planner and keepsake

Oxmoor House®

ISBN-13: 978-0-8487-3489-3
ISBN-10: 0-8487-3489-0
Library of Congress Control Number: 2011935844

Printed in China
First Printing 2012

Oxmoor House
VP, Publishing Director: Jim Childs
Editorial Director: Susan Payne Dobbs
Creative Director: Felicity Keane
Senior Brand Manager: Daniel Fagan
Senior Editor: Rebecca Brennan
Managing Editor: Laurie S. Herr

Southern Living Wedding Planner and Keepsake
Editor: Susan Hernandez Ray
Project Editor: Emily Chappell
Senior Designer: Melissa Clark
Production Manager: Greg Amason

Southern Living®
Editor: M. Lindsay Bierman
Copy Chief: Susan Emack Alison
Project Manager, Special Issues: Paden Reich
Assistant Production Manager: Christy Coleman
Associate Garden Editor: Rebecca Bull Reed

Contributors
Writers: Maria Cooke, Kelly Seizert
Designer: Blair Gillespie
Photographer: Kate Headley
Copy Editors: Rebecca Benton,
    Norma Butterworth-McKittrick
Proofreaders: Dolores Hydock, Carmine Loper
Indexer: Mary Ann Laurens
Interns: Laura Hoxworth, Alison Loughman
Calligrapher: Allison Banks

Time Home Entertainment Inc.
Publisher: Richard Fraiman
VP, Strategy & Business Development: Steven Sandonato
Executive Director, Marketing Services: Carol Pittard
Executive Director, Retail & Special Sales: Tom Mifsud
Executive Director, New Product Development:
    Peter Harper
Director, Bookazine Development & Marketing:
    Laura Adam
Publishing Director: Joy Butts
Finance Director: Glenn Buonocore
Assistant General Counsel: Helen Wan

To order additional publications, call 1-800-765-6400 or 1-800-491-0551.

For more books to enrich your life, visit **oxmoorhouse.com**

Contents

Foreword

Congratulations—you're engaged! As a Southern bride-to-be, you are about to embark on a journey that you will remember and cherish forever. Whether you've been dreaming of this day for years or you've just gotten started, you have made a very important step (other than saying "yes!"). Buying a wedding planner is essential to staying organized and keeping all of your ideas in check. Let's face it: Planning a wedding is hard work, and balancing friends, family, and a fiancé is no small feat!

At *Southern Living,* our goal is to make the planning process easier on you—so you can spend more time dreaming and less time stressing. That's why we teamed up with two of the best Southern wedding planners in the business, Maria Cooke and Kelly Seizert of Ritzy Bee Events in Washington, D.C. From choosing venues to setting a budget, these women are full of real-world advice. Whether you're planning an affair for 50 or 500, Maria and Kelly will help you get started and stay on track.

Best wishes, and happy planning!

Jessica

Jessica S. Thuston
Executive Editor, *Southern Living*

Welcome

He popped the question. You said, "*Yes!*"

Standing at the starting line of wedding planning comes with a wide array of emotions, ranging from absolute excitement and anticipation of all the fun decisions you have ahead of you, to quite a bit of stress when you stop and realize *how many* decisions are ahead of you.

Reading and referencing this wedding planner is the start to helping you stay on the bridal bliss track from now until you reach the end of the aisle on your wedding day. Chapter by chapter, you will be guided on ways to approach all of your decisions with confidence, while hopefully having fun along the way. Flipping through the pages, we hope you will be inspired with ideas and beautiful photographs of Southern weddings. "Words of wisdom" are planning tips sprinkled throughout the chapters with helpful reminders and hints. Note sections can be used to jot down your wedding wants and whims. Storage pockets are for you to tuck away all of the ideas you collect, as well as important vendor information and contracts, keeping your wedding organized in one pretty place.

Whether you have been dreaming your whole life about making these plans, or you've simply been looking forward to creating a meaningful day for the two of you, we hope this planner will stay on your shelf for years to come and represent a fond keepsake of your wedding planning journey.

So now that you've said, "*I will,*" it's time to prepare to blissfully say, "*I do!*"

Best planning wishes,

Kelly Seizert & *Maria Cooke*

Kelly Seizert & Maria Cooke
Ritzy Bee Events

Best wishes

You are about to embark on an adventure as you plan a wedding! For many engaged couples, the wedding day is the start of a new beginning. The day celebrates everything that brought the couple together and builds anticipation for what the future holds.

Whether you are the bride, the groom, or a family member or friend helping with the festivities, this planner will guide you through the wedding-planning world and the wedding day one step at a time.

Using the Planner

Your engagement is an exciting time, but it can also be rather over-whelming as you figure out how to get started with the planning process. Whether you have been engaged for one hour or one year, this planner will help you make the most of your time before the big day. The chapters are designed to help you focus on each element, task, and decision at a manageable pace.

If you are early in the planning process, major preparation steps may take place concurrently. For example, if you know you want to be married in a church, you may be wondering if you should pick the venue or the date first. Keep in mind that either decision affects the other, so you may want to make them at the same time.

Some decisions will need to happen in order. For example, you will need to know the shape, dimensions, and quantity of dinner tables before selecting table linens to be sure they are available in the size and quantity you need.

With other decisions, you can have flexibility to come back to them later in the process. For example, you will book a band or DJ early in the process, but you won't need to submit an overall song request list to them until a month or two prior to the wedding.

Keep track of all the details in this step-by-step guide that you'll want to take with you everywhere. And one day, you can look back on the journey that led up to a day that was uniquely yours. But, in the mean-time, relax and enjoy this once-in-a-lifetime experience.

Getting Started

Before you get started, keep these tips in mind to help you maintain perspective on what might seem like a daunting list of to-dos:

- **Set aside a specific time to do your planning.** Maybe it is a Saturday morning or a weekday evening. Do not cram your planning and phone calls in between meetings at work. Make time when you can really focus on the task at hand.

- **Decide whom you want to be a part of your planning process, and stick with those individuals.** Entrust those who will give you positive support and will encourage you to make the wedding about the two of you. Everyone will have an opinion, so involving all of your family and friends in your decision-making process will lead to more stress and confusion. If a particular person, like a sister or your future mother-in-law, insists on being involved and taking charge, consider selecting a smaller responsibility you are willing to let go of, such as sourcing the products that will go into guest welcome bags. Let that person do the research for you, and then you can give the final nod of approval.

- **Organization is key.** Create an organized space to keep your ideas, magazine tear sheets, contracts, and other wedding-related documents. We've included pockets in the planner to help you keep track of these things. Keep soft copies of lists and spreadsheets on your computer, and keep hard copy documents in this planner so you can easily access everything.

- **Subscribe to a few sources of inspiration.** You will find endless inspiration on wedding and design blogs and also inside the pages of wedding magazines. Use these sources to collect ideas, styles, and colors that catch your eye.

- **Keep perspective.** At the end of the wedding day, the food will be eaten, the band will play its last song, and guests will go home with fond memories of an amazing event. As important as all of the wedding planning details will seem, it helps to remember that the celebration goes beyond the wedding day and is truly about the two of you and your marriage to each other.

Example of a Planning Scenario

- **Style:** An early-summer garden party with guests mingling in suits and cocktail dresses.

- **Setting:** Ceremony in the garden at a private estate, cocktails by the pool, and a plated dinner in an adjacent tent.

- **Size:** 200 guests or less.

- **Spending:** Bride's parents handle the majority of costs, while groom's parents host the rehearsal dinner. Bride and groom pay for the band and honeymoon.

Defining Expectations

The first step in the planning process is to determine what type of wedding you would like to have. It's important to define what the expectations are for the affair so that each vendor involved, element contracted, and detail designed fits your wants and needs. To begin, let yourself dream about what your day is going to be like in terms of the Four Ss—Style, Setting, Size, and Spending—and try to picture yourself in each scenario.

Style: Is it a formal event? Is it more casual? Is it a daytime or evening affair?

_____

_____

_____

_____

_____

Setting: Are you inside a church? A hotel ballroom? In a garden? On a family farm? On an exotic island?

_____

_____

_____

_____

_____

Size: Is it purposefully more intimate with only close family and friends, or is it 400 friends? Or maybe it's somewhere in between?

_____

_____

_____

Spending: How does your budget come into play with your vision? What is your budget?

_____

_____

_____

_____

Defining Your Buzz Words

Once you have defined your Four Ss, move on to creating your list of your top 10 Buzz Words. They can be anything! When listed, your Buzz Words will create an index-style narrative of the details, emotions, and overall vision you hope to experience on your wedding day. These words will serve as a "guide" of sorts to help direct you in making decisions that fit with your vision. And they will come in handy when you begin the process of describing your wedding wishes to potential vendors.

Examples of Buzz Words

1. timeless
2. detailed
3. romantic
4. blush tones
5. sophisticated
6. Southern hospitality
7. live music
8. alfresco dining
9. lush flowers
10. seersucker suits

My Buzz Words:

1. _____
2. _____
3. _____
4. _____
5. _____
6. _____
7. _____
8. _____
9. _____
10. _____

Laying the Foundation for Planning

Inevitably, you will want to jump directly into planning the really fun details of the wedding, such as looking for the dress and selecting what flowers you will carry. But before you do anything else, two major planning steps need to be defined—the size of your budget and the size of your guest list. These directly correspond to all other plans you will make, and they also equally affect each other. Taking a logical approach to your wedding on the front end will let you enjoy selecting the details later in the process.

The Budget

Approaching the wedding-budget discussion with your fiancé and family should be the VERY first thing you do. Schedule a time you can sit down together as a group and have an open conversation about what everyone is able to financially contribute toward the wedding. If your fiancé's family has also offered to contribute to the overall wedding budget, include them in the discussions as well.

The "who pays for what" standards have changed in the past few decades. No longer is the bride's family automatically expected to take on the entire expense of the wedding. Tradition still encourages the bride's family to host the wedding and the groom's parents to host the rehearsal dinner, but there are no set rules for wedding funding. If you and your fiancé are paying for your own wedding, carefully discuss what your finances will allow, and then stick to a strategy of what you can comfortably spend.

Budget-planning Tips

- **Prioritize your investments.** While you are creating your budget and assigning dollars to the different categories, keep in mind what items are most important to you so that you allocate dollars appropriately. If photography is a priority and you want to splurge on an experienced photographer who will capture your moments perfectly, you might be willing to hire a local DJ versus a more notable band to balance out your costs.

- **Spend wisely.** Yes the day is about the two of you, but it is also very important to consider your guests' experience. If you have a $30,000 wedding budget and spend $15,000 on your wedding dress, it is unreasonable to ask and expect your guests to cover the cost of their drinks with a cash bar just because you overspent in a category.

- **Cushion your budget.** It is almost a guarantee that things will cost more than you think they will. Plan on spending about 10 percent more than what you estimate on the front end.

- **Look for ways to save.** Inviting fewer guests is the number one way you will save money. You also might consider an alternative to a sit-down dinner reception, such as having a wedding brunch or lunch. Scheduling your wedding on a Friday or Sunday is another way to give you the advantage of being able to negotiate with venues and vendors a bit because they are less in demand. Also consider utilizing family and friends who have appropriate skill sets. For example, you might have a friend who is a graphic designer by trade and is willing to work with you on designing your invitations. Or maybe you have a cousin who plays guitar and would be happy to provide your ceremony music.

- **Be thankful.** Last, but not least, be appreciative and considerate of what family members are willing to contribute. Remember, nobody should be going into years of debt as a result of the wedding.

Although it's not the fun part of planning, it is essential that you sit down early in the process to set a solid financial plan with your fiancé and family members. This will help you get clear expectations so you can move forward and feel comfortable making decisions that align with your budget.

details, details, details

Before you decide about tipping, you will want to check your contracts to see if gratuity is already included. If it's not included in the contract, you might consider adding it to the contract just so you will not have to worry about it on the big day.

As a general guide, you don't tip owners. For example, if the baker who makes your cake owns the business, then you wouldn't tip him or her. You may want to give a tip or a small gift to someone who has gone the extra mile for you, such as a photographer who takes additional time for some candids that you really love. Place the money in an envelope, and pass it to the vendor just before he or she leaves.

General Tipping Guides:

Wait staff: between 15 and 20 percent of the total catering bill

Catering manager: $200

Bartenders: between 10 and 20 percent of the total liquor bill

Coat check attendants: $1 to $2 per guest

Bathroom attendants: $1 to $2 per guest

Hair stylist: 15 to 20 percent

Limo driver: 15 percent

Musicians: 15 percent

Officiants: a $100 to $400 donation to the church

Sample Wedding Budget Worksheet

Here is an example of how this budget template may be used for you to organize your own wedding estimates.

Sample Wedding Budget Worksheet

Category	Item	Vendor	Description	Estimated Cost	Actual Cost	Who is Paying?
Ceremony	*Site fee(s)*	St. Matthew's Church	church & organist fees	$500		Groom's parents
Ceremony	*Officiant fee*	Rev. Smith	donation	$200		Groom's parents
Ceremony	*Marriage License fees*	State Marriage Bureau	application & processing fees	$75		Groom
Reception Venue	*Rental fee*	Peach Grove Manor	10-hour rental	$10,000		Bride's parents
Reception Venue	*Insurance*	WedSafe	required liability coverage from venue	$250		Bride's parents
Food & Beverage	*Beverages (alcohol & non-alcohol)*	Love at First Bite Catering	for 200 guests	$6,000		Bride's parents
Food & Beverage	*Food for cocktail hour, dinner & dessert*	Love at First Bite Catering	for 200 guests	$25,000		Bride's parents
Food & Beverage	*Service charge & tax*	Love at First Bite Catering	20% SC + 6% tax	$8,060		Bride's parents
Cake	*Cake design, delivery & tax*	Cakes by Carin	$5.00 per slice $200 delivery 6% tax	$1,260		Bride
Rentals	*Chairs, tables, linens, specialty furniture, etc.*	Event Rental Services	$7.00 per chair, $45 per linen, 30 tables, lounge seating collection	$3,750		Bride's parents
Rentals	*Dance floor*	Event Rental Services	20 X 20 black & white checkered dance floor	$1,800		Bride's parents
Rentals	*Delivery, labor & tax*	Event Rental Services	$500 delivery/ labor & 6% tax	$833		Bride's parents
Stationery	*Wedding Web site*	Webwed	private site with security	$45		Bride
Stationery	*Save-the-dates*	PrettyPaper	115 flat printing	$345		Bride's parents

Sample Wedding Budget Worksheet

Category	Item	Vendor	Description	Estimated Cost	Actual Cost	Who is Paying?
Stationery	*Invitations & inserts*	PrettyPaper	Letterpress with map, weekend itinerary & response card inserts	$1,725		Bride's parents
Stationery	*Postage for save-the-dates & inserts*	UPS + Ebay	Mix of vintage stamps & regular	$200		Bride
Stationery	*Calligraphy*	Fancy Writing	Invitations ($4) & escort cards ($2)	$860		Bride
Stationery	*Day-of paper products: program, escort cards, place cards, menus, table numbers, signage*	Fancy Writing	Programs & menus letterpress and escort cards & table numbers flat printed	$2,400		Bride's parents
Photography	*Photographer's fees*	Snap Shot	8-hour coverage, assistant package	$5,000		Bride
Photography	*Album(s)*	Snap Shot	1 regular & 2 parents	$2,500		Bride + Groom
Floral	*Bridal bouquet*	Blooms	Seasonal flower assortment	$250		Bride's parents
Floral	*Bridesmaids' bouquets*	Blooms	$100 each X 4 girls	$400		Bride's parents
Floral	*Groom & Groomsmen*	Blooms	$15 X 5 boutonnieres	$75		Bride's parents
Floral	*Additional personal for parents, grandparents & children*	Blooms	2 nosegays for moms, 2 boutonnieres for dads, 1 corsage for grandmother, flower girl hair wreath	$150		Bride's parents
Floral	*Ceremony decor*	Blooms	2 altar plinths & 8 aisle markers	$550		Bride's parents
Floral	*Cocktail hour decor*	Blooms	$45 X 8 cocktail tables	$360		Bride's parents

Sample Wedding Budget Worksheet

Category	Item	Vendor	Description	Estimated Cost	Actual Cost	Who is Paying?
Floral	*Reception decor*	Blooms	$250 X 20 table centerpieces, $300 escort card table display	$5,300		Bride's parents
Floral	*Delivery fees, labor & tax*	Blooms	Delivery/labor is 10% of total + 6% tax	$1,133.60		Bride's parents
Music & Entertainment	*Ceremony music*		Already under church fees			Bride's parents
Music & Entertainment	*Cocktail hour music*	Spring Strings	String quartet for an hour	$500		Bride's parents
Music & Entertainment	*Reception music*	The Groove	5-piece band	$4,500		Groom
Lighting	*Lighting, labor, delivery & tax*	Action Lights	Pin spotting dinner tables	$3,025		Bride's parents
Tent	*Tenting, labor, delivery & tax*	Canopy Co.	60 X 80 with sidewalls & fans	$6,000		Bride's parents
Decor & Details	*Favors & favor packaging*	Wrap Up	Jars & tags only, Grandma's jam (no cost)	$300		Bride
Decor & Details	*Out-of-town welcome gifts*	Wrap Up & Cost Mart	Snacks in kraft boxes for $10 X 75	$750		Bride + Groom
Decor & Details	*Non-floral tabletop decor: candles, candle holders, etc.*		Frosted votives & candles included with caterer			Bride's parents
Decor & Details	*Ceremony: unity candle, ketubah, etc.*	TBD		$500		Bride's parents
Decor & Details	*Reception: guestbook, toasting flutes, cake cutter/ server set, etc.*	TBD		$500		Bride's parents

Sample Wedding Budget Worksheet

Category	Item	Vendor	Description	Estimated Cost	Actual Cost	Who is Paying?
Decor & Details	*Miscellaneous*			$1,500		Bride's parents
Transportation	*For bride & groom*	Vintage Ride	Gold Bentley from church to reception	$450		Groom
Transportation	*For bridal party & guests*	Shuttles For Hire	To/from hotels to church & reception	$3,000		Groom's parents
Hotel Room	*Bride & groom hotel stay for wedding night*	Peach Tree Inn	Bride staying Friday night & wedding night in hotel room	$675		Groom
Wedding Planner	*Service fees*	Wedded Bliss	Month of planning package	$2,000		Bride
Attire	*Wedding dress*	Bridal Boutique		$5,000		Bride's parents
Attire	*Wedding dress alterations*	Bridal Boutique		$500		Bride's parents
Attire	*Accessories: shoes, veil/ headpiece, jewelry, purse, trousseau*	Miscellaneous		$1,000		Bride
Attire	*Wedding rings*	Jewel Box	Pavé band + white gold band	$3,000		Groom
Attire	*Groom's attire*	Miscellaneous	Custom suit	$1,000		Groom
Hair & Makeup	*Wedding day & pre-wedding trial(s)*	Peach Tree Inn Spa		$500		Bride

Wedding Budget Worksheet

Category	Item	Vendor	Description	Estimated Cost	Actual Cost	Who is Paying?
Ceremony	*Site fee(s)*					
Ceremony	*Officiant fee*					
Ceremony	*Marriage License fees*					
Reception Venue	*Rental fee*					
Reception Venue	*Insurance*					
Food & Beverage	*Beverages (alcohol & non-alcohol)*					
Food & Beverage	*Food for cocktail hour, dinner & dessert*					
Food & Beverage	*Service charge & tax*					
Cake	*Cake design, delivery & tax*					
Rentals	*Chairs, tables, linens, specialty furniture, etc.*					
Rentals	*Dance floor*					
Rentals	*Delivery, labor & tax*					
Stationery	*Wedding Web site*					
Stationery	*Save-the-dates*					

Wedding Budget Worksheet

Category	Item	Vendor	Description	Estimated Cost	Actual Cost	Who is Paying?
Stationery	Invitations & inserts					
Stationery	Postage for save-the-dates & inserts					
Stationery	Calligraphy					
Stationery	Day-of paper products: program, escort cards, place cards, menus, table numbers, signage					
Photography	Photographer's fees					
Photography	Album(s)					
Floral	Bridal bouquet					
Floral	Bridesmaids' bouquets					
Floral	Groom & Groomsmen					
Floral	Additional personal for parents, grandparents & children					
Floral	Ceremony decor					
Floral	Cocktail hour decor					

Wedding Budget Worksheet

Category	Item	Vendor	Description	Estimated Cost	Actual Cost	Who is Paying?
Floral	*Reception decor*					
Floral	*Delivery fees, labor & tax*					
Music & Entertainment	*Ceremony music*					
Music & Entertainment	*Cocktail hour music*					
Music & Entertainment	*Reception music*					
Lighting	*Lighting, labor, delivery & tax*					
Tent	*Tenting, labor, delivery & tax*					
Decor & Details	*Favors & favor packaging*					
Decor & Details	*Out-of-town welcome gifts*					
Decor & Details	*Non-floral tabletop decor: candles, candle holders, etc.*					
Decor & Details	*Ceremony: unity candle, ketubah, etc.*					
Decor & Details	*Reception: guestbook, toasting flutes, cake cutter/ server set, etc.*					

Wedding Budget Worksheet

Category	Item	Vendor	Description	Estimated Cost	Actual Cost	Who is Paying?
Decor & Details	*Miscellaneous*					
Transportation	*For bride & groom*					
Transportation	*For bridal party & guests*					
Hotel Room	*Bride & groom hotel stay for wedding night*					
Wedding Planner	*Service fees*					
Attire	*Wedding dress*					
Attire	*Wedding dress alterations*					
Attire	*Accessories: shoes, veil/ headpiece, jewelry, purse, trousseau*					
Attire	*Wedding rings*					
Attire	*Groom's attire*					
Hair & makeup	*Wedding day & pre-wedding trial(s)*					

Building Your Guest List In Excel:

Start an Excel spreadsheet as your guest-list tracker. Use these categories as column headers so it is easy to merge, sort, and stay organized with your lists. This will also help later when assigning tables and writing escort cards, place cards, and even thank-you notes.

Categories include:

- guest of bride or groom
- salutation, first name, and last name
- full mailing address
- e-mail address
- "save-the-date" mailed
- invitation mailed
- RSVP for wedding, food selection, special dietary request
- total number attending
- names of attendees
- wedding-table number
- hotel name
- wedding gift item
- thank-you note sent

The Guest List

Part of laying the foundation for the wedding-planning process is determining the number of guests that your wedding budget will allow. Before you start personally inviting everyone you know, carefully think through what an attainable number will be.

- Start making a list of guests you would like to invite, and ask your fiancé to do the same. Decide if you want single guests (those not married, engaged, or seriously dating someone) to bring a guest. Consider if you are going to include children on the guest list. And don't forget to include the most important people of all—the two of you!

- Ask parents from your side and his side to also make their lists and to rank the priority of those guests. This is a good time to set some parameters if you feel they are needed. For example, family aside, you may ask your parents to only invite their close friends whom you also know well and not the neighbor down the street whom you have never met but your mom sees at book club every other month.

- Merge all the lists together, and remove the inevitable duplicates to see where your numbers fall. More likely than not you will need to start trimming the list and prioritizing your "must invite" list.

- Avoid making a "B" list. It is tempting to think you can set aside a group of potential guests, such as co-workers, and only invite them if you get declines from your "must invite" list. However, this can backfire and appear rude if you cannot give those guests enough notice to plan to attend.

- Inevitably there will be a few tough discussions on individuals who are questionable invitees. And it can be downright emotionally taxing to debate whether or not second cousins should be invited or if children will be included. Take the approach of deciding which battles are worth fighting and which are not—and what decisions might be worth making to keep relationships harmonious.

Determining the Date and Selecting the Venue

In order to create a timeline and book vendors, you need to set a date. Easy, right? Well, the process can be a little more complicated than it might seem. First decide whether you will have the ceremony and reception in the same location. For couples who are only searching for one venue, the search for the right place will be a bit more streamlined. Couples who are looking for a ceremony and reception in two different locations have a few more decisions to make. Here are some tips to help you set the date.

General Venue Considerations

■ **What are you looking for in a venue?**
   Ex: An inside or outside space? Catering in-house? A specific type of decor?

■ **How does your "ideal date" fit with your budget?**
   Ex: Are you potentially paying a premium to marry on a Saturday evening during a busy month, or could you stretch the value and wed on a Friday night during a slower period?

■ **Will the space accommodate all of your guests?**

■ **What's included with the space you are hoping to secure?**
   Ex: Does the venue provide tables and chairs? Does the church provide the ceremony musicians?

■ **Will the potential venue hold a date without a fee?**

■ **What is the reservation and deposit process?**

■ **Will you need to provide additional structures to make the space usable?**
   Ex: Do you need a tent, generator, lighting, air conditioning/heat?

■ **Is there a preferred vendor list? Will you need to pay a fee should you wish to use a vendor not on the list?**

One location:

■ **What is the ceremony space like? Will you need to re-use certain spaces?**
   Ex: Will you have to "flip" the ceremony space to create the dinner space while guests are enjoying cocktails in a separate area?

■ **Will your wedding be the only wedding there that day?**

Two locations:

■ **Do you need to be "active members" of the church in which you wish to marry?**

■ **Are you willing to let go of the ceremony location if the reception venue is not available or vice versa?**

Defining Your Style

Maybe you have imagined your wedding day in narrative detail from the time you were a child. Or perhaps the only detail you know for sure is that you want your partner at the end of the aisle. Regardless of your mindset, designing and constructing the stylized details of your day is a fun but challenging task. As you begin the process of marrying your budget with the details you envision, keep in mind that a wedding should always reflect you as a couple and your love and influences. And, just like relationships, there is almost always a little give and take.

To begin designing your day, think about the weddings you've attended. List the things that you liked about them and the things that you would have changed. What elements felt too over the top? Which ones were not enhanced enough? And most importantly, what details did you remember? Next, have a look at your list of Four Ss—Style, Setting, Size, and Spending—and at the budget you established. Ask the tough question: "What wedding can we afford to host?"

With the brainstorm under way, move on to gathering images that will inspire your design process. If you have not yet explored the world of wedding details, browse magazines, blogs, and books in search of ideas that fit with your list of Four Ss. As you flip (or scroll) the page, be on the lookout for general concepts that evoke the "I love that!" response.

Surprisingly, it can be just as helpful to see what you do not like if you need help defining your style. Do not hesitate to collect a group of pictures that represent things you do not want.

make it yours

When you've gathered what you feel is a solid selection of ideas that best represent the style you envision for your day, you may choose to take one extra step and pull your ideas into an Inspiration Board. You can do this on your computer or simply cut and paste existing images onto a piece of paper. The goal is to end up with a one-page arrangement of photos that depict the mood, touch on the details, and tell the story of your day.

Examples of Style

1. Coastal
2. Contemporary
3. Glam
4. Green
5. Kitschy
6. Modern
7. Retro
8. Rustic
9. Shabby Chic
10. Theme
11. Timeless
12. Traditional

Examples of Details To Look for:

- **Color Combinations:** Colors you like, colors you don't like, main and accent colors

- **Fabrics, Fonts, Patterns, and Phrases:** Smaller details that enhance

- **Stationery:** "Save-the-date" and invitation designs, menu cards, escort cards, table numbers

- **Ceremony:** Location options, chair arrangements, aisle and altar decorations, traditions

- **Attire:** Gowns, attendants' apparel, accessories, going-away outfits

- **Flowers:** Bouquet shapes, centerpieces, boutonnieres/corsages, accent arrangements

- **Details:** Favors, unique touches, send-off options, table decor, unique guest book options, and escort card displays

- **Cuisine:** Cake styles, shapes, and flavors; menu ideas; specialty drinks

SPRING
{Peony, Celery, Bluebird}

FALL
{Burlap, Pumpkin, Harvest}

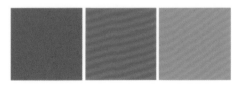

SUMMER
{Lemonade, Lime Peel, Strawberry Patch}

WINTER
{Cranberry, Evergreen, Snow Globe}

Where to Look

Inspiration is everywhere! You may find design ideas for your wedding from a variety of sources. If you are not the type to take out a sketchbook and make ideas happen from the pen and paper, don't worry! There are plenty of existing resources just waiting to be found. Begin by taking some time to explore your local bookstore and the Internet to see what catches your eye. Here are a few sources that are overflowing with ideas.

■ **Your local super store:** The paint-supply section of any hardware or specialty store is a wonderful source for free inspiration. The endless displays of swatch cards offer instant inspiration for foolproof color combinations. Swatch cards are generally free to take, and since these cards tuck neatly in this folder, be sure to grab a few of each color so you can leave them with friends, family, and vendors as a reference. These cards also offer a great resource on color palettes. To avoid a "matchy-matchy" look, use a range of color intensities. Also, don't forget to take a stroll down the cosmetics aisle. From makeup palettes to nail polish displays, you never know what color will catch your eye!

words of wisdom: A Pantone swatch book (available online and at most fine art-supply stores) is a great resource for color combinations. PMS, or the Pantone Matching System, is a precise guide and internationally recognized resource that provides the exact "recipe" for each color. PMS defines color not by a clever name but rather by number. Referencing a Pantone shade when selecting your colors will ensure a nearly exact match. This is especially helpful when working with invitation designers.

Bridal magazines: As you've probably already found out, there are lots of bridal magazines on newsstands. Some are national publications, while others cater to specific regions and states. It is a good idea to select a few magazines that offer different perspectives on style, decor, trends, vendors, and additional planning tips. As much as you probably want to buy one copy of every publication, use restraint and purchase just a few at a time. It is very easy to become overwhelmed with the eye candy that the glossy pages provide.

Fashion, design, and popular culture magazines: If you step beyond the bridal section of the newsstand, you are bound to bump into the fashion, design, and popular culture magazines. Don't pass by them too quickly, as they are a wonderful source for guidance on general design and color trends. You may be very surprised where you find inspiration! It may come from the colors used in a shoe advertisement, the typeface of a recipe, or even the "general feeling" of a room shot. Unlike with magazines specifically focused on weddings, you will need to use your imagination to help translate the inspiration you take from an everyday item to make it aisle-worthy.

Blogs: The world of wedding blogs is unending. There are a variety of nationally known blogs that provide up-to-the-minute ideas, tips, photos from real weddings, and even do-it-yourself (DIY) projects. A simple Google search for "wedding blogs" will return a tremendous number of options. To navigate this online world, begin perusing a few blogs that catch your eye, and check each site for other blogs. As you visit each blog, remember to bookmark your favorites and subscribe to their RSS feed for updates delivered straight to your e-mail inbox whenever they publish new content. Blogs are great for finding ideas from actual weddings. Most often submitted by the couple's photographer, the pictures will let you peek at real weddings, from the getting-ready shots to the getaway car. Unlike with a magazine, you can't tear out a page from the Internet, so be sure to print any good ideas or copy the pictures into your folder on your computer desktop.

words of wisdom: Take advantage of sites that offer free e-mail addresses by creating an e-mail address specifically for wedding correspondence. It will help keep your vendor correspondence and blog updates organized in one place. By keeping your personal, work, and wedding contact e-mail addresses separate, you won't find yourself in the middle of a meeting and getting instantly distracted when wedding-related e-mails come in.

Wedding Blogs for Inspiration

100LayerCake.com

Brooklyn Bride, bklynbrideonline.com

ClassicBride.blogspot.com

From-i-will-to-i-do.blogspot.com

GreenWeddingShoes.com

GreyLikesWeddings.com

InspiredBride.net

JunebugWeddings.com

MerciNewYork.blogspot.com

MerrimentEvents.com

OhSoBeautifulPaper.com

OnceWed.com

PerfectBoundBlog.com

RitzyBee.com

RuffledBlog.com

Snippet & Ink, snippetandink.com

StyleMePretty.com

TheBridesCafe.com

TheSweetestOccasion.com

WeddingBee.com

WeddingChicks.com

With-this-ring.blogspot.com

Your Planning Timeline

10 months or more

☐ Secure a wedding planner if you are planning to use one, and decide how much assistance you need (full planning, partial planning, or month-of services).

☐ Brainstorm about your day—develop your list of Four Ss and Buzz Words for guidance.

☐ Have a meeting with the "finance committee" (groom and family members) to establish a budget.

☐ Draft an initial guest list to determine how many guests you could have in attendance (keeping in mind the budget you set).

☐ Research and secure ceremony and reception locations.

☐ Formally set the date (with your officiant if in a place of worship and/or with your ceremony/reception venue).

☐ Draft an Inspiration Board with mood, style, and decor ideas.

☐ Begin researching vendors that fit your budget and style. Book any vendors you know are an immediate fit.

☐ Select a bridal party.

☐ Make appointments to try on bridal gowns.

☐ Have an engagement party.

☐ Select a resource for "save-the-dates," or select a custom stationer.

8-10 months

☐ Book a caterer (if needed).

☐ Book a photographer.

☐ Book a florist.

☐ Book your musical entertainment for the reception.

☐ Book a tent vendor (if needed). They can help you with lighting, flooring, power, etc.

☐ Purchase a bridal gown.

☐ Research bridesmaids' dresses and mothers' attire.

☐ Start a registry.

☐ Create a wedding Web site.

☐ Finalize your guest list spreadsheet with full names and correct addresses.

☐ Secure a calligrapher for addressing needs.

☐ Order "save-the-dates" and postage.

☐ Start a contact list for all your vendors (and keep adding to it).

☐ Start a calendar of payment deadlines, and adjust as you go.

6-8 months

☐ Secure a hotel room block for out-of-town guests.

☐ Mail "save-the-dates."

☐ Book a transportation company.

☐ Book a videographer.

☐ Book a cake baker.

☐ Book ceremony music.

☐ Make an appointment at a rental company to select and order table linens, chairs, etc.

☐ Research and discuss honeymoon options.

☐ Meet with your caterer to discuss menu options.

☐ Purchase bridesmaids' attire.

☐ Purchase your veil, shoes, trousseau, jewelry, and other accessories.

☐ Secure a hair stylist and makeup artist.

4-6 months

☐ Purchase or rent groom/groomsmen's attire.

☐ Book your honeymoon.

☐ Have your menu tasting with your caterer.

☐ Write your ceremony. Select and notify participants in the ceremony.

☐ Meet with your florist to finalize floral arrangements.

☐ Begin any DIY projects.

☐ Adjust guest list, if necessary, and order invitations and postage.

☐ Have a bridal shower.

☐ Have a trial run with your hair stylist and makeup artist.

2-4 months

☐ Determine who will be speaking at the reception.

☐ Select key songs (first dance, father-daughter dance, mother-son dance, cake cutting, last dance).

☐ Take a dance lesson(s).

☐ Write your wedding day/weekend agenda.

- [ ] Have invitations calligraphed.
- [ ] Mail invitations.
- [ ] Have a dress fitting.
- [ ] Make arrangements for pets and house sitting for the time you are away on your honeymoon.

1 month

- [ ] Apply for a marriage license.
- [ ] Sort through RSVPs.
- [ ] Draft seating charts and table assignments.
- [ ] Adjust floral proposal based on final floor plan (if needed).
- [ ] Distribute final wedding agenda and contact list to vendors.
- [ ] Send song list to DJ/band.
- [ ] Hold a final walk-through at the venue with all of your vendors.
- [ ] Have your final dress fitting.
- [ ] Have your final hair cut/color.
- [ ] Hold a bachelorette/bachelor party.

2 weeks

- [ ] Organize, box, and label all decor items.
- [ ] Assemble bride's wedding day "emergency" kit.
- [ ] Give final guarantee to caterer. (Be sure to alert them to any dietary restrictions.)
- [ ] Print final guest list (by alphabetical order and table assignment), and distribute to vendors.
- [ ] Send escort cards to the calligrapher.

- [ ] Make final calls to all of your vendors, and review contracts and details. Pay any outstanding balances.

1 week

- [ ] Pack for your honeymoon.
- [ ] Pack clothing for your wedding weekend events.
- [ ] Pick up your wedding dress.
- [ ] Assemble hotel welcome bags.
- [ ] Schedule any bills that are due while you are away.
- [ ] Deliver all decor and personal items to your wedding planner or venue.
- [ ] Confirm the transportation schedule.
- [ ] Assemble tips in envelopes for each vendor necessary.

The Day Before

- [ ] Check into your hotel. Leave an extra room key at the front desk for any vendors needing access to your room.
- [ ] Deliver welcome bags to hotel(s) prior to arrival of out-of-town guests.
- [ ] Host a bridal luncheon for your attendants.
- [ ] Get a manicure and pedicure.
- [ ] Pack your handbag for the wedding day; lay out shoes, accessories, etc.
- [ ] Attend the wedding rehearsal.
- [ ] Have fun at your wedding rehearsal dinner.
- [ ] Get a good night's sleep!

The Wedding Day

- [ ] Eat breakfast and lunch.
- [ ] Move your engagement ring to a different finger.
- [ ] Take your time getting ready.
- [ ] Be sure any payments due to vendors are prepared and distributed.
- [ ] Trust your hired vendors to execute and manage your day.
- [ ] Remember to hand off your going-away outfit or luggage to the designated person.
- [ ] Relax and enjoy!

Post-Wedding

- [ ] Reconcile with any outstanding vendor balances.
- [ ] Return all rental equipment (if not picked up on the wedding day).
- [ ] Change your name on all legal documents (if necessary).
- [ ] Have your gown cleaned and preserved.
- [ ] Write thank-you notes.

Sample Wedding Day Agenda

8:00 A.M. WEDDED BLISS arrives onsite at Inn
EVENT RENTAL SERVICES delivers
rentals + dance floor

9:00 A.M. ACTION LIGHTS installs tent lighting

10:30 A.M. PEACH TREE INN places linen + sets
tables

11:00 A.M. HAIR + MAKEUP begins at the Spa

2:00 P.M. BRIDESMAIDS arrive dressed to
Anna's suite
BLOOMS delivers personal flowers
SNAP SHOT arrives at Peach Tree Inn

2:15 P.M. Getting ready shots
Anna steps into her gown

3:00 P.M. BLOOMS delivers floral to church
THE GROOVE arrives at Inn for setup
"FIRST LOOK" pictures at Inn on dock

3:15 P.M. SHUTTLES FOR HIRE arrive at Inn with
shuttle #1
VINTAGE RIDE Rolls Royce arrives at Inn

3:45 P.M. WEDDED BLISS arrives at church
ST. MATTHEW'S CHURCH ready for
guests
BRIDAL PARTY departs for church

4:00 P.M. BRIDAL PARTY pictures at church
ST. MATTHEW'S CHAMBER TRIO sets up
SHUTTLES FOR HIRE ready with shuttles
at Inn to take guests to church
BLOOMS delivers reception floral to tent

4:15 P.M. SHUTTLES FOR HIRE depart Inn with
guests

4:30 P.M. GROOMSMEN in place to escort guests
FIRST GUESTS arrive at church
ST. MATTHEW'S CHAMBER TRIO begins
CAKES BY CARIN delivers cake
SPRING STRINGS arrive at Inn to set up

4:50 P.M. LAST GUESTS arrive at church

4:55 P.M. ST. MATTHEW'S CHAMBER TRIO last
song of prelude

5:00 P.M. CEREMONY BEGINS
<<Song change: Air on G>>

SEATING OF THE MOTHERS
John's mother escorted by his father
Anna's mother escorted by Michael
<<Song change: Jesu, Joy of Man's Desiring>>

5:03 P.M. REVEREND, JOHN, + GROOMSMEN ENTER
(this order: John, Matt, Josh, Tom, Paul)

5:06 P.M. BRIDESMAIDS ENTER
(this order: Ginny, Suann, Kate, Lauren)

5:09 P.M. RING BEARER ENTERS - Issac

5:10 P.M. FLOWER GIRL ENTERS - Jaden
<<Song change for bridal processional:
Canon in D>>

5:12 P.M. ANNA + HER FATHER ENTER

5:15 P.M. SERVICE BEGINS
Words of Welcome
Sentences of Scripture
Gift of Marriage
Declarations of Intent
Affirmations of the Families
Affirmations of the Congregation
Reading
Exchange of Vows
Exchange of Rings
Prayer
The Lord's Prayer
Pronouncement of Marriage
Charge and Blessing

5:30 P.M. SHUTTLES FOR HIRE ready at church
THE GROOVE live sound check at Inn

5:40 P.M. CEREMONY ENDS/BRIDAL PARTY
RECESSES <<Song: Spring>>
SNAP SHOT + IMMEDIATE FAMILY take
pictures at church (1 shuttle to stay behind)
SHUTTLES FOR HIRE depart church for Inn

Cocktails to End:

6:00 P.M. PEACH TREE INN ready for guests
SPRING STRINGS ready in cocktails
COCKTAILS begin

6:45 P.M. GUESTS CALLED TO DINNER
THE GROOVE playing light music

7:10 P.M. ANNA + JOHN INTRODUCED head right
to dance floor (no bridal party introductions)
"Mr. and Mrs. John Marshall"
FIRST DANCE
<<Song: Someone Like You>>

7:15 P.M. WELCOME TOAST by Anna's dad

7:20 P.M. FIRST COURSE SERVED
Light music playing

7:35 P.M. PARENT DANCE (shared)
<<Song: Stand By Me>>
Anna + Dad go first then welcome
John + Mom

7:40 P.M. FIRST COURSE CLEARED

7:55 P.M. ENTRÉE SERVED
THE GROOVE (15 min. break)

8:10 P.M. THE GROOVE returns

8:25 P.M. BEST MAN SPEECH (Matt)

8:30 P.M. MAID OF HONOR SPEECH (Lauren)
(followed by a 30 +/- minute dance set)

9:00 P.M. CAKE CUT BY ANNA + JOHN
<<LIGHTING CHANGE>>

9:05 P.M. DANCING RESUMES

10:00 P.M. PEACH TREE INN to pass late night snack
BLUE SKY FILMS done

10:45 P.M. BARS CLOSE

10:55 P.M. LAST DANCE
<<Song: Don't Stop Believing>>

11:00 P.M. EVENT ENDS

Floor Plan:

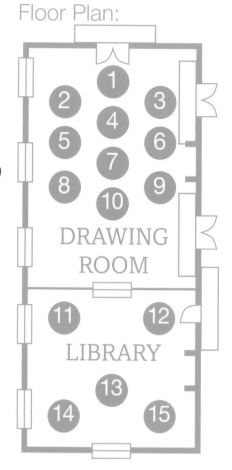

*Vendor meals count: 5

Table 1/9 seats
Table 2/8 seats
Table 3/10 seats
Table 4/10 seats **parents of the groom**
Table 5/9 seats
Table 6/7 seats
Table 7/8 seats **parents of the bride**
Table 8/8 seats
Table 9/9 seats
Table 10/10 seats
Table 11/10 seats
Table 12/10 seats
Table 13/10 seats ****A+J here****
Table 14/10 seats
Table 15/10 seats

Your Wedding Day Agenda

Start-of-day thru Ceremony:

Time: Notes:

Ceremony:

Time: Notes:

Reception:

Time: Notes:

Floor Plan:

Diagram:

Notes:

_____

_____

_____

_____

_____

_____

_____

_____

_____

_____

_____

_____

_____

_____

_____

_____

_____

_____

_____

Contracts

Each chapter of this planner will address specific category guidelines and questions to ask your potential wedding vendors as you interview them to be a part of your wedding day team. As vendors begin to submit proposals and contracts to you, carefully check all language and wording in the contracts to be sure all information is accurate. Things to look out for:

- Make sure that the wedding date, location names, and location addresses are correct.

- Check to see that the bride and groom's names are spelled correctly, as well as parents' names if parents are signing off as the contracting party.

- Confirm that contact information is correct for not only you but also for any designated contact vendors could reach out to on your wedding day should you not be available (or not want to be disturbed).

- Be sure vendors note the correct start/end times of the wedding and also understand the times they are permitted to begin setup, as well as the amount of time they have for breaking down and cleaning up after the wedding.

- Make certain that payment deliverable dates are clearly noted on the contracts. Typically, all vendors will require a deposit when you book, and the remaining balance will be due on or prior to the wedding date.

- Be sure to understand the terms you are agreeing to should your wedding date need to change or be canceled.

- Confirm that all of your vendors can adhere to the ceremony and reception venues' policies and restrictions.

- Make certain your vendors can provide the insurance and permits required.

- Be sure to review any specific requirements in their contract language, such as vendor meals, breaks, rider specifications, and logistical and technical needs.

Notes:

Wedding Insurance

Typically there are two types of wedding insurance (also called "event insurance"): cancellation insurance and vendor-required liability insurance. Some homeowner's policies will allow for coverage, and there are also dedicated insurance companies that offer wedding-day protection coverage.

Cancellation insurance protects your financial investment in the wedding and can help cover cancellations, postponements, lost deposits, stolen gifts, no-show vendors, and even damages to property.

Vendor-required liability insurance: Liability policies protect the venue and contracting party from damages to property, alcohol-related accidents, or bodily injury to guests attending. Although not required by all wedding venues, some will require the contracting party to provide a certificate of insurance showing the individual has liability coverage in a minimum required amount. This is often in addition to the individual wedding vendors that are also responsible for providing their own proof of insurance.

Shopping for
The Dress

For many brides, the idea that they are preparing to be married doesn't quite register until they are in front of a bridal-salon mirror in a gorgeous white gown. The quest for the perfect dress is over in a matter of minutes for some brides, while others require months of searching. Regardless of your shopping style, make sure you take the time to enjoy this once-in-a-lifetime experience.

Your wedding dress should be an extension of your personality and should reflect the way you want to present yourself on your special day. It is an important factor in making you feel beautiful. And because your wedding photographs will last beyond your lifetime, consider how your wedding day look will appear years from now. Do you want to be a time-less bride with a look that transcends generations? Or would you prefer to exude stylish appeal that reflects the year's iconic fashion trends?

What to Expect

Allow yourself as much time as possible to look for your dress. Once your dress is ordered, it can take an average of six to eight months for it to arrive at the salon. You will then need two or three fittings to get the dress looking perfect. In addition to keeping the timeline in mind as you search for your dress, also remember that wedding dress styles are different from ready-to-wear clothing. While you might shy away from a certain neckline or fabric in your day-to-day attire, remain open-minded when trying on gowns. Brides are often pleasantly surprised with the styles they thought they would have never tried on.

It's okay if you don't know what you want in a bridal gown when you start your search. But it does help to have an idea of how you want to feel. If you are at a loss for words when it comes to describing dress details that catch your eye, try and communicate to your consultant your answers to these questions:

- What are your wedding Buzz Words (page 14)? What is the mood of the day?

  _____

  _____

- How do you want to feel on your wedding day (timeless, modern, flirty, demure, etc.)?

  _____

  _____

- What physical characteristics of your body do you love?

  _____

  _____

- What physical characteristics would you prefer to gently distract attention from?

  _____

  _____

- Would you like to include any heirloom pieces in your finished look?

  _____

  _____

details, details, details

Being Prepared for Your Appointment:

❁ Wear nice (but modest) undergarments

❁ Bring a good strapless bra (just in case the salon doesn't provide one)

❁ Take along a shoe with the heel height you'll most likely wear with the dress

❁ The day of your appointment, style your hair and apply soft makeup. It will help you better envision your overall look.

❁ Bring your Buzz Words (page 14) and Inspiration Board (page 32): Feel free to show it to your consultant if you think it might better describe the look you are trying to achieve.

Shopping

The journey of finding the dress of your dreams may be over when you try on your first gown, or it may involve a longer search and a bit more patience. Here are a few questions to ask yourself and tips to keep in mind to help you make the most of this important and emotional shopping experience.

Before You Go

- **Do your homework:** Look online and at bridal magazines for pictures of dresses that catch your eye. Tear the pictures out and keep them in this binder for reference.

- **Research salons:** Decide what type of salon fits your personality:

  ☐ *A small local salon with a well-curated collection of couture designers?*

  ☐ *A New York City flagship showroom featuring the work of just one designer?*

  ☐ *A large salon with a variety of price points and designers from which to choose?*

  ☐ *A more budget-friendly chain where you can leave with a gown in hand?*

  ☐ *A local seamstress who will make your gown from scratch?*

  ☐ *A "one-stop shop" that carries everything from undergarments to gowns to bridesmaids' accessories?*

- **Set a budget maximum:** Everyone has a budget. Ask yourself at what price point you will feel uncomfortable putting down the plastic.

- **Make an appointment:** Most salons require a formal appointment made well in advance. Try to be flexible with your schedule, as Saturday appointments fill up quickly.

- **Ask the receptionist:** Inquire if there is anything specific you need to bring with you. And ask her how many people the dressing rooms can comfortably accommodate.

■ **Set the salon up for success:** If your body type makes shopping for clothing somewhat of a challenge, let the salon know in advance. Perhaps you are especially petite or require more support for your enviable curves. Sharing this information from the start will help the salon be prepared.

■ **Assemble your support:** If you think you would like a support team, ask a few key people whose company you enjoy and opinions you trust to accompany you. Do NOT bring an entourage. You may think you want a bonding experience and the opinions of your 12 bridesmaids, but trust us—just like accessories, less is more.

■ **Decide whose opinions are most important:** If your parents are buying your dress, will they get to weigh in on your decision? Will you always have the final say?

During the Appointment

■ **Arrive on time:** Bridal salons are busy places, so it is important to allow yourself plenty of time for your scheduled appointment. Running late can lead to rushed decisions.

■ **Check your self-consciousness at the door:** It's more common than not that your consultant will accompany you into the dressing room. If you think you may feel uncomfortable, remember to wear undergarments with a bit more coverage.

■ **Think beyond the hanger:** Bridal fashion is very different from ready-to-wear. Trust in your consultant's abilities to know what designers, dress shapes, and fabrics will make you look your best. Try not to judge a dress by how it looks on the hanger.

■ **Clearly state your budget:** Whether you have limited funds or unlimited options, it's important to tell your consultant where you draw the line. There is nothing worse than falling in love with a dress you simply can't afford.

■ **Don't be a label snob:** There are so many talented designers available to brides today! Try not to let your perception of what you "should" wear influence your decision. After all, your guests will be looking at you, not the label inside your dress.

■ **Be ready to use your imagination:** Sample bridal gowns come in a limited variety of sizes and are adjusted to fit your shape with utility clips and closures. Be understanding of the fact that you may have to look beyond these fasteners to really see the dress of your dreams.

■ **Be honest with your consultant:** Let her know your true opinions of the styles you try on. (She won't be offended, we promise!)

■ **Communicate body-image goals:** Hoping to increase your workout schedule during your engagement? Does stress affect your jean size? Let your consultant know of your plans so they may size your dress accordingly.

■ **Ask about alterations:** Does the salon offer them? How much will they cost?

■ **Take notes:** Most salons will not let you snap photos until you have signed your sales contract, so keep detailed notes on what you liked and what you didn't care for (see the dress scorecards on page 60).

Dress Shopping Scorecard

Take this worksheet with you to wedding
salons to remember dresses you try on.

Salon: _____

Visit Date: _____

Consultant: _____

Dress Name/Number: _____

_____

Designer: _____

Style/Cut: _____

_____

Fabric: _____

Distinguishing Details: _____

_____

_____

Likes: _____

_____

_____

Dislikes: _____

_____

_____

Score: 1 2 3 4 5 6 7 8 9 10

Price: _____

Notes: _____

_____

_____

_____

_____

Dress Shopping Scorecard

Take this worksheet with you to wedding
salons to remember dresses you try on.

Salon: _____

Visit Date: _____

Consultant: _____

Dress Name/Number: _____

_____

Designer: _____

Style/Cut: _____

_____

Fabric: _____

Distinguishing Details: _____

_____

_____

Likes: _____

_____

_____

Dislikes: _____

_____

_____

Score: 1 2 3 4 5 6 7 8 9 10

Price: _____

Notes: _____

_____

_____

_____

_____

Dress Shopping Scorecard

Take this worksheet with you to wedding salons to remember dresses you try on.

Salon: _____

Visit Date: _____

Consultant: _____

Dress Name/Number: _____

_____

Designer: _____

Style/Cut: _____

_____

Fabric: _____

Distinguishing Details: _____

_____

_____

Likes: _____

_____

_____

Dislikes: _____

_____

_____

Score: 1 2 3 4 5 6 7 8 9 10

Price: _____

Notes: _____

_____

_____

_____

_____

Dress Shopping Scorecard

Take this worksheet with you to wedding salons to remember dresses you try on.

Salon: _____

Visit Date: _____

Consultant: _____

Dress Name/Number: _____

_____

Designer: _____

Style/Cut: _____

_____

Fabric: _____

Distinguishing Details: _____

_____

_____

Likes: _____

_____

_____

Dislikes: _____

_____

_____

Score: 1 2 3 4 5 6 7 8 9 10

Price: _____

Notes: _____

_____

_____

_____

_____

Finding The Dress

For many brides, the *knowing* feeling that they have found the perfect wedding dress is one of quiet confidence. Others are overcome when they find the right gown. Here are a few tips to help you when your consultant asks, "Is this dress a yes?"

If you are ready to purchase:

- Have your measurements taken.

- Pay the deposit.

- Take some pictures for reference: This will help when it comes to shopping for accessories. (Be sure to take full-length, close-up, and detail shots of the fabric, adornments, etc.)

- Define the next steps: Set follow-up appointments.

- Keep in touch: Be sure to get your consultant's business card.

If you need some time to think:

- Thank your consultant: Be honest about your plan. ("I want to keep looking" or "I'd like to sleep on it.")

- Follow up: Make another appointment to try on the top contenders again.

- Be courteous: If you decide to buy elsewhere, let the runner-up salons know.

After your appointment:

- Accessorize: Begin searching for pieces to complement your dress. You'll need to have undergarments and shoes selected before your first fitting.

- Attend fittings: When your dress finally arrives, you'll be called back into the salon for your fittings. Be sure to bring your undergarments and shoes with you so the seamstress can alter your gown to the correct measurements. Also bring along the person who will be in charge of bustling your dress. Take step-by-step pictures and notes, as some bustles can be quite complicated.

make it yours

Trunk Shows Can Let You Customize

A trunk show is a special event held at a bridal salon where a designer typically appears, or sends a representative, to show off his or her collection. Salons often offer you a discount if you purchase your dress that day. Trunk shows are great opportunities to see new collections and to get personal suggestions from the designer on what type of veil to wear with your gown. Some designers are even willing to make design changes to suit your style.

Dress Styles

A-line	Ball Gown	Empire
At the top of the list for a reason—it's the most flattering silhouette of all, with its slimming and forgiving effects. Generally slim on top and through the waist and gradually flares away from the body like the shape of the letter "A." If you have more curves, ask for a modified A-line.	A romantic cut with a small waist and a voluminous skirt.	A high, raised waist hitting just under the bust. The skirt may be straight or slightly flared.
Flattering on: Almost all body types.	*Flattering on:* Those who need curves and those who have curves. Best on those of average height who are not too short and petite.	*Flattering on:* Small busts and petite figures.

Mermaid	Sheath	Short	Trumpet
Typically fitted long and snug to the knees and then flares out.	This body-hugging shape outlines every curve.	Short dresses have a hem above or just slightly below the knee.	Similar to a mermaid shape. Body-hugging at the top and through the hips but flares out into a fuller skirt at the bottom.
Flattering on: Those who are short and those who are short-waisted.	*Flattering on:* Tall, slim, and petite figures.	*Flattering on:* Most shapes, depending on the cut and fabric. A short dress is for an informal wedding or as a dress the bride will change into during the reception.	*Flattering on:* Petite figures and those who want to show off curves.

Necklines

Bateau	Cowl	Halter	High Neck
A "boat neck" top that follows the curves of the collarbone to the tip of the shoulders. Elongates the neck.	Extra material around the neck makes the garment hang in a soft "U" shape that ends around the chest.	Straps that wrap around the back of the neck. Typically on backless gowns.	A neckline that sits high or even wraps around the neck like a collar. Enhances the bust, so not recommended for bigger busts.

Jewel (or T-shirt)	Off the Shoulder	One Shoulder	Portrait
A high, circular neckline around the entire neck.	Sits below the shoulder and highlights the collarbone and shoulders. Flattering for wider hips.	A strap going across one shoulder that creates an asymmetric look and enhances small busts.	Similar to a bateau with the neckline standing or flaring out to form a mini collar effect that frames the upper chest.

Notes: _____

_____

_____

_____

_____

_____

_____

_____

_____

Necklines

Scoop	Sheer	Spaghetti Strap	Square
A "U" shaped neckline.	A sheer layer of fabric or lace that is typically paired with a sweetheart neckline.	Thin straps that frame shoulders. Complements narrow shoulders.	A straight bodice with right angles at the straps.

Strapless	Sweetheart	V-neck	Queen Anne
No straps. Typically straight across or with a slight curve up or down.	Shaped like the top of a heart. Offers a great way to enhance curves.	A "V" shaped neckline that extends down.	A high-rising collar at the back of the neckline with a lower neckline across the chest.

Notes: _____

_____

_____

_____

_____

_____

_____

_____

Waistlines

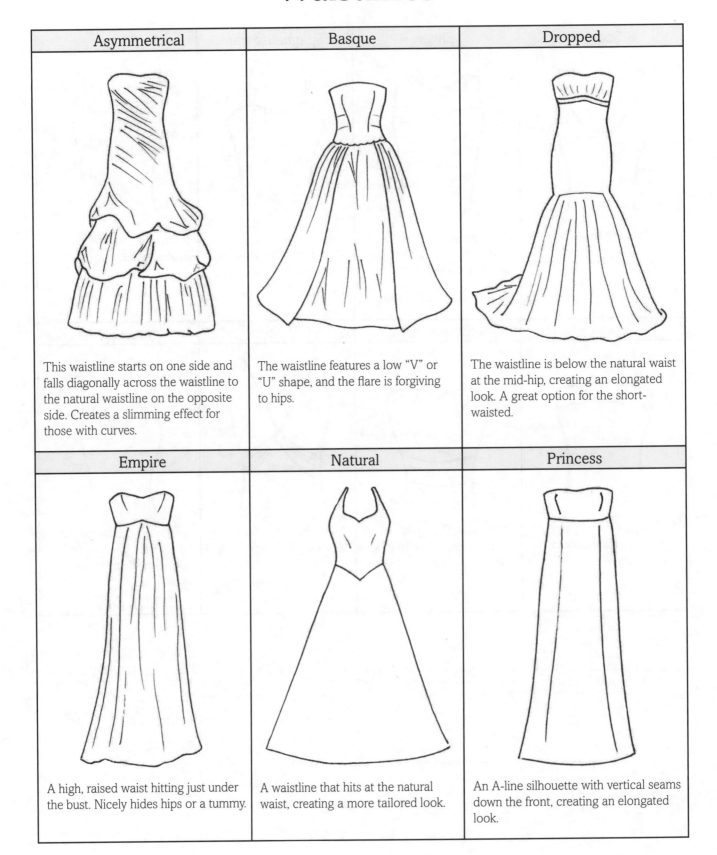

Asymmetrical	Basque	Dropped
This waistline starts on one side and falls diagonally across the waistline to the natural waistline on the opposite side. Creates a slimming effect for those with curves.	The waistline features a low "V" or "U" shape, and the flare is forgiving to hips.	The waistline is below the natural waist at the mid-hip, creating an elongated look. A great option for the short-waisted.
Empire	Natural	Princess
A high, raised waist hitting just under the bust. Nicely hides hips or a tummy.	A waistline that hits at the natural waist, creating a more tailored look.	An A-line silhouette with vertical seams down the front, creating an elongated look.

Sleeves

Bell	Cap	Fitted	Flutter
Long or short; flares toward the bottom.	A very short sleeve that covers the shoulder.	Long sleeves that hug arms all the way to the waistline.	Short sleeves that are loose and create a ruffled look.

Illusion	Poet	Sleeveless	T-shirt
A sheer fabric that gives the illusion of no sleeves.	Long sleeve fitted from the shoulder to the elbow and flaring out toward the bottom.	No sleeves.	A short sleeve that looks similar to the sleeves of a T-shirt.

Notes: _____

_____

_____

_____

_____

_____

_____

Trains

Cathedral	Chapel	Court
Formal and long.	Formal but still versatile.	A less formal and shorter option than the chapel or cathedral.
Length: Typically 6 – 7½ feet	*Length:* Typically 3 – 4 feet	*Length:* Typically 1 – 2 feet

Fishtail	Sweep	Watteau
The shortest train that flares out from the knee.	Barely "sweeps" the floor. The back hem is only a few inches longer than the front hem.	Attaches at the mid-back and falls to the floor.
Length: Typically no more than 1 foot	*Length:* Typically no more than 1 foot	*Length:* 3 – 4 feet

Do the Bustle!
Your bridal salon alterations
attendant will discuss and design
a specific bustle for your dress,
if needed, at one of your fittings.
Be sure to bring along your
maid of honor—or anyone
else who will be present on the
wedding day to bustle your
dress for you.

Veils and Headpieces

Wearing a veil sets such a romantic tone and is a distinct symbol of wedding tradition. Veils range from the understated to the dramatic, and there are more than a dozen styles from which to choose.

When choosing a veil, be sure the fabric will complement the dress style and fabric. The veil should not compete with any details of the dress. Also consider your ceremony location. Some settings, such as a windy beachside venue, are not conducive to a bride comfortably wearing a long veil.

words of wisdom: Most veils attach with a headpiece such as a comb. When removing the veil, typically before your entrance into the reception, be sure to designate your maid of honor or someone similar to help you carefully remove the veil and store it somewhere safe.

Birdcage	Blusher	Cathedral	Double Tier
A shorter style made with netting and often accessorized with a jeweled piece or whimsical detail like feathers.	A single layer that is worn over the face during the ceremony. It can be paired with a longer veil or worn by itself.	The longest and most formal of veil lengths.	A veil that has layers extending to two different lengths to create more volume.
Elbow	Fingertip	Floor-length	Pouf
A popular choice for casual weddings. Connects to the headpiece and extends to the elbows.	Typically the most compatible of veils with almost any dress style. Extends to the fingertips.	Extends to and sweeps the floor.	Folded at the crown or back of the head.
Mantilla	Waltz	Waterfall	
A traditional "Spanish" style. Drapes over the head and does not require a headpiece since it is pinned to the hair.	Extends from the headpiece to the ankles. More commonly worn with dresses that don't have a train.	Cascading edges in varying lengths.	

Veil alternatives:

❋ Adorned headbands from Jennifer Behr. Visit jenniferbehr.com/index.php

❋ Heirloom clips or combs from an antique jewelry store

❋ Flowers worked into your hair individually or as a wreath created by your florist

❋ A statement piece like an oversized silk flower

Fabric Glossary

Brocade (also called Jacquard): Heavy fabric with a complex weave or pattern.

Charmeuse: Lightweight type of satin; semi-lustrous with great drape.

Chiffon: Delicate, sheer, and transparent, with a soft finish. Often layered because of its transparency.

Crepe: Sheer and lightweight with a crinkled surface and great drape.

Duchesse Satin: A lightweight blend of silk or polyester and rayon woven into a satin finish.

Dupioni: A textured silk with a finish similar to Shantung, but with thicker fibers and a slight sheen.

Faille: A silk or blend fabric with a ribbed pattern texture that resembles grosgrain ribbon.

Georgette: A sheer and lightweight fabric with a crepe surface.

Organza: A structured material that holds shape well and has a dull luster.

Satin: A heavier but smooth fabric with a high sheen on one side and matte reverse.

Shantung: A lightweight woven silk, similar to a raw silk and characterized by its rough texture.

Taffeta: A crisp, smooth, structured fabric made from silk.

Tulle: Fine and delicate netting.

Lace glossary

Alencon: A delicate needlepoint with both pattern and netting.

Eyelet: Woven clusters of holes with stitching around the holes.

Chantilly: Delicate and small floral motifs on netting.

Guipure: Heavier, raised patterns in needlepoint that are sewn together onto netting.

Point d'esprit: Round or oval dots on sheer netting.

Accessories

Once you have found the perfect dress and veil or hair accessory, it's time to have fun with selecting the remainder of your outfit.

Shoes

Admit it, second to the wedding dress search, you've probably been investing quite a bit of time looking for the perfect shoes to accompany your dress! For many brides, justifying investing in an amazing pair of shoes is easy since this will be the most important outfit you will ever wear.

Before you go on your quest for the perfect pair, consider these tips:

- **Comfort:** No shoe, no matter how amazing or beautiful, is worth wearing if it feels painful. You'll be on your feet and dancing for hours, and you'll thank yourself for adhering to this tip!

- **Height:** Be sure you have your shoes with you at final wedding dress fittings to ensure they will work. Also consider your fiancé's height.

- **To heel or not to heel:** Consider if you are comfortable walking in heels, especially in the setting you will be in. If you are getting married on a farm, for example, you certainly do not want your heels sinking into the ground all day.

- **Take two:** Consider purchasing a lower heel or cute flats to change into at a later point if you do not think you can make it the entire day in heels.

- **Repurpose:** If your wedding shoes are a splurge, consider their purpose post wedding: Can you really wear them again?

Jewelry

Although it may be a few hours into the day, you will be sporting the most important (and symbolic) piece of jewelry on your wedding day—your wedding ring! Lucky for you, this day is also a chance to put on some sparkle you might not normally wear.

Things to keep in mind when considering jewelry:

■ **Consider your overall outfit:** If your dress has embellishments like beading or an intricate jeweled detail, do not overwhelm the rest of you with too much sparkle.

■ **Use jewelry to balance out your look:** If you are wearing a strapless gown, consider statement earrings or a necklace. If you are wearing a high neckline, avoid too much on top and wear a beautiful bracelet on a bare arm. Less is definitely more with wedding day jewelry!

■ **Family jewels:** Only wear a family heirloom or gift if it works with your attire. Make sure it is properly insured prior to wearing it.

■ **Put a ring on it:** Only wear your engagement and wedding ring on your fingers.

Bags

You won't need to carry much on your wedding day (that's what bridesmaids are for!), but carrying a small clutch or handbag is a nice way to tote the essentials, such as your ID, cash, mints, and lip gloss.

Gone are the days of carrying a bag that matches your wedding dress. Whether it has embellished details or it is a vintage piece, the bag should enhance the overall style and feel you are trying to create!

Wraps & cover-ups

No matter in which season you are getting married, take the time to find and purchase a seasonally appropriate cover-up piece. Fall and winter brides have fun options to choose from, ranging from a beautiful cashmere sweater to a fur jacket or stole. Spring and summer brides should consider a lightweight wrap that can be easily toted by a bridesmaid.

Southern touch

Many Southern brides also carry handkerchiefs that have been passed down from generation to generation. They can be monogrammed with initials from the various brides who have carried them.

Trousseau

{trous·seau} n. The possessions, such as clothing and linens, that a bride assembles for her marriage.

Rising in popularity in the Victorian era, a bride's trousseau consisted of items of fanciful clothing, fine linens, jewelry, and accessories gathered and gifted by the bride's family that the bride would need and use throughout her marriage. These items were most commonly presented and kept in a hope chest. A well-appointed trousseau served as a symbol of status, as it was filled with only the finest of textiles and jewels.

Today's interpretation of a modern trousseau loosely refers to the items that the bride-to-be will wear to specific engagement festivities and wedding day events. It also includes items she will take on her honeymoon.

■ **Party Attire:** Throughout your engagement, you may be invited to an engagement party, bridal shower, or rehearsal dinner in your honor. Just like other parties you've attended, it is important to dress accordingly. Take clues from the invitation itself and the time of day the event is taking place. If the invitation outlines the desired dress code, do your best to select a well-thought-out outfit to help you put your best foot forward. It is not uncommon for the bride to wear a short white party dress to pre-wedding events. Many bridal designers are offering different versions of "the little white dress." Also, styling yourself for a wedding-related party is a perfect time to incorporate some of the trends that you may not have decided to incorporate into your wedding day look!

words of wisdom: If you are planning a garter toss, look for a designer who makes a "garter pair." This allows for one to be a "tossing garter" and the other to be kept as a keepsake.

Wedding Dress Undergarments: We all know that even supermodels have their tricks to making them look like, well, supermodels. Ask your bridal consultant what pieces you need to make your wedding dress look its best. A corset-style strapless bra, seamless undies, and the tried-and-true Spanx™ are just a few behind-the-scenes pieces that will make you look amazing. Regardless of what garments you opt to put in your "support and smoothing" arsenal, keep in mind that you still want to be comfortable. Look for well-constructed pieces in shades close to your skin tone. And, blushing aside, let's be honest—we all know these support pieces are probably not what you had in mind when you thought of what you'd wear on your wedding night. So, while you are shopping, pick up something that you do think you and your new husband will enjoy. When the reception is over and you have retired to your room, you'll welcome the change of clothing!

Lingerie: These are the most commonly gifted items in a modern trousseau. Do not be surprised to receive some rather intimate apparel at your bridal shower or bachelorette party. For some ladies, the idea of opening a negligee in front of guests is downright mortifying, while for others it is chalked up to tradition. Either way, be gracious! After all, a close friend or relative gifted it with you in mind.

Not all bridal showers deliver lingerie. If you want to create or add to your own trousseau, don't be shy! Head to a local specialty store or the intimates section of a department store to browse. Try on different pieces until you find something that looks and feels great. If your taste is a bit more understated and simple, a silk slip or satin robe are some versatile pieces to keep in your closet.

Honeymoon Attire: Don't forget about your honeymoon! While most brides do not need to buy a whole new wardrobe for their travel, you may use your trip as an excuse to fill a few gaps in your closet. Be sure to purchase and pack pieces that layer easily and may be mixed and matched. Look ahead to find out what the climate will be like, and make yourself aware of any social customs.

details, details, details

Lingerie Bags

If you don't already own some, be sure to purchase a few lingerie bags. These simple drawstring (or zipper) bags are made of breathable cotton and sized to hold your intimate apparel. They come in handy when packing your suitcase and have been known to keep your undies organized and your blushing to a minimum during those predictable TSA searches at the airport. You might also invest in a waterproof bag for your bathing suit.

Bridesmaids

So much has changed in the world of bridesmaids' dresses! Long gone are the days of puffy taffeta and dyed-to-match satin shoes. For the modern bride and her attendants, the world of bridesmaids' attire is filled with fresh and fashion-forward options, available in almost any fabric and at almost every price. As you play stylist to your bridal party VIPs, remember that your favorite ladies will look their best if they feel confident in the dress you select!

Before you make an appointment to try on bridesmaids' dresses, do a little homework to help you prepare. First, decide how involved you want to be. Are you planning to select a dress on behalf of all of your attendants? Will you offer some guidance and then hand off the shopping duties to your maid of honor? Regardless of what direction you take, begin with your Buzz Words (page 14) and have your Inspiration Board (page 32) in hand to help describe how you would like your ladies to look. Try to form your own unique answers to the following questions. Then, with your answers defined, you can ask your attendants for their input.

- [ ] Do you prefer a more formal or informal style?
- [ ] Do you have a lot of different body types, heights, and complexions to dress?
- [ ] Do you envision all of your attendants in the same style dress?
- [ ] How do you feel about mixing fabrics, colors, or styles?
- [ ] Do you envision the dress or the accessories serving as a focal point of the "look"?
- [ ] Are you planning to use fashion to distinguish your maid or matron of honor?
- [ ] What will the weather be like?

Bridesmaids' Style Card

Copy and send this worksheet to all of your bridesmaids so they can keep track of their attire details.

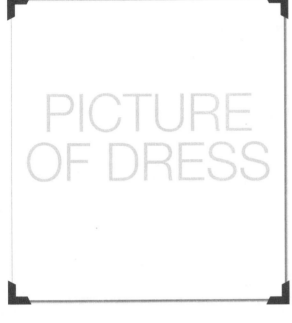

Brand: _____

Web site: _____

Style name: _____

Fabric/color: _____

Shoe brand/style: _____

contacts

Salon name: _____

Consultant name: _____

Salon phone: _____

Seamstress name: _____

Seamstress phone: _____

Hair stylist/salon: _____

Salon phone: _____

Makeup artist/salon: _____

Salon phone: _____

measurements

Height: _____

Bust: _____

Waist: _____

Hips: _____

Dress size ordered: _____

Shoe size: _____

important dates/times

Wedding: _____

Date dress ordered: _____

Alteration appointment: _____

Hair appointment (wedding day): _____

Makeup appointment (wedding day): _____

payments

Deposit amount/date: _____

Balance due/date: _____

Alterations: _____

Cost of shoes: _____

Cost of accessories: _____

Hair style fee/tip: _____

Makeup fee/tip: _____

purchased

☐ Dress   ☐ Shoes   ☐ Undergarments   ☐ Accessories

Budget

Setting a budget for bridesmaids' dresses is important, whether you are the one footing the bill or if you are asking each attendant to purchase her own dress.

If you are paying for the dresses:

☐ Decide how much per dress you can afford to spend.

_____
_____
_____

☐ Decide whether you will also be paying for their accessories.

_____
_____
_____

If your attendants are paying for their own dresses:

☐ Ask each girl how much she would feel comfortable investing.

_____
_____
_____

☐ Consider the other costs that might be associated with your wedding: Does each bridesmaid need to travel a great distance to celebrate with you? Is she also in a lot of other weddings?

_____
_____
_____

words of wisdom: If you want to give your attendants a color reference and swatches are not available, head to the paint store. Paint chip cards are free!

Shopping Tips

■ **Save the "group shopping" for later:** Start out with just your maid of honor, and see what looks appeal to both of you. Let her try on dresses and give your honest feedback. When you are able to narrow the options down to a few great contenders, schedule an appointment for the entire group. Fewer opinions will help you stay stress-free.

■ **Bring your Buzz Words (page 14):** And your Inspiration Board (page 32)! Just like when you were shopping for bridal gowns, these tools will help relay your ideas about your day to the consultant, making it easier to reach decisions that fit with the big picture.

■ **Consider what complements:** Look for dresses that complement your bridal gown. You want the entire feel of your bridal party to be cohesive and stylish.

■ **Leave plenty of time:** Bridesmaids' dresses usually take 3 to 4 months to produce. Ask the salon for ordering suggestions to be sure your dresses arrive with time for needed alterations.

■ **Plan for physical changes:** Not every one of your attendants will still look exactly the same when shopping for dresses and on your wedding day. Plan to be flexible and accommodating for ladies who know they will be expecting or decide to change up their hairstyles.

■ **Be generous:** Accepting the title of "maid of honor" or "bridesmaid" comes along with a variety of emotional, financial, and time-consuming responsibilities. Be certain to show your genuine thanks and make each girl feel special. If each attendant is paying for her own dress, perhaps offer to give the coordinating accessories as gifts.

■ **Decide if you are willing to compromise:** What will you do if your attendants all love one dress but you love a different one?

■ **Put it in writing:** Help your attendants remember the important information by filling out the Bridesmaids' Style Card (see form on page 81).

Notes:

Makeup and Hair

Although the bridal glow is a perfect start, having great makeup and hair will only help you feel more ready to be in the spotlight on your big day. Finding the right makeup artist and hair stylist to achieve your look is key! Begin your search for your beauty dream team by looking at samples of their past wedding work and by gathering references.

Things to keep in mind:

- When you begin discussing your day with these stylists, start to think about the location where you will be getting ready. You will need to discuss whether you will have to go to the salon or if they will come to you. If they come to you, be sure to figure out if there is enough space, natural lighting, and electric outlets to power styling tools.

- Schedule a trial appointment for hair first, and then move on to scheduling your makeup trial after you know what your hairstyle will be. Bring ideas of styles and makeup examples you love from wedding and fashion magazines and other places of inspiration.

- Bring your veil or any hair accessory with you to the hair trial so you can have a true vision of what you will look like.

- Be sure to discuss any allergies you might have to makeup, and try the exact products they will be using on you for the big day. The last thing you would want is to break out in a rash on your wedding day! Also discuss with your makeup artists any products that have the potential to reflect flash from cameras, causing you to appear discolored.

- If you are happy with your trial(s), move forward with booking both vendors.

- Start to discuss with your beauty vendors how much time it will take them to work on you and on any of the ladies in the wedding party having services done.

- Poll your wedding party (and family members) on who would also like to take part in beauty services. Provide the ladies with any special instructions they need to follow.

Wedding Day Beauty Schedule

Organize your wedding party's hair and makeup schedules for the wedding day and give all of the ladies a copy of the final itinerary.

Please arrive by:_____

"Getting Ready" location:_____

Stylist: _____

Location: _____

Start time	End time	Name	Up-do, Blowout, etc.

Stylist:_____

Location: _____

Start time	End time	Name	Up-do, Blowout, etc.

Dress and Beauty "Emergency Kit"

You will want to have some dress repair tools and beauty essentials with you the entire day just in case. Put a bridesmaid in charge of keeping these products with her so they are readily available to you (or any of the other ladies) should you need them.

☐ Aspirin or pain reliever

☐ Baby wipes (for cleaning hands)

☐ Bandages

☐ Blister treatment

☐ Blotting paper

☐ Bobby pins (in various hair colors)

☐ Breath mints

☐ Brush & comb

☐ Chalk (helps to mask stains)

☐ Clear nail polish and the nail polish color you will be wearing

☐ Cotton balls

☐ Cotton swabs

☐ Crochet hook (for fastening buttons)

☐ Deodorant

☐ Emery board

☐ Fabric-friendly fashion tape (for holding "things" in place)

☐ Hairspray

☐ Hem or fabric tape

☐ Lint roller

☐ Makeup products you will be wearing for the wedding

☐ Mouthwash

☐ Mirror

☐ Nail polish remover

☐ Safety pins

☐ Small sewing kit with a needle, threads that match your dress and the bridesmaids' dresses, and buttons

☐ Stain-remover wipes

☐ Tissues

☐ Tums

☐ Tweezers

words of wisdom: Put an extra pair of appropriately colored men's socks in the bride's wedding day emergency kit just in case one of the guys forgets his pair!

Groom and Groomsmen

While it's true that all eyes will be on the bride, don't let your groom and his attendants go unnoticed. For some guys, fashion is a part of their everyday lives, while others will be happy with you giving the direction on what they wear. When you begin the search for the formalwear that will help your groom put his best foot forward, remember that it is important for the entire bridal party to have a style that is cohesive yet complementary. And, just like with the wedding dress, there are many options available to today's grooms that extend beyond the basic black-and-white tuxedo. Regardless of what your husband-to-be selects, remember that a timeless look will suit a gentleman forever.

Formal Wedding

	Clothes	Accessories
Daytime	black or gray cutaway coat, gray striped trousers, formal white dress shirt with wing collar	ascot or four-in-hand tie, black socks, black patent shoes, black silk hat (optional)
Evening (after 6 p.m.)	black tailcoat with matching trousers, piqué wing-collar shirt	white bow tie and vest (piqué), black socks, black shoes, white gloves, black silk hat (optional)

Semiformal Wedding

	Clothes	Accessories
Daytime	oxford gray stroller coat with gray striped trousers, white shirt with turned-down collar	striped four-in-hand tie, black shoes, black socks
Evening (winter)	black tuxedo jacket with matching trousers, vest, white dress shirt with turned-down collar	white bow tie and vest (piqué), black socks, black shoes, white gloves, black silk hat (optional)
Evening (summer)	white tuxedo jacket with black trousers, cummerbund, white dress shirt	black socks, black shoes, bow tie

Groom and Groomsmen Attire

Athletic Cut	Slim Cut	Navy Blue Blazer/Khakis

Groomsmen:

_____   _____
_____   _____
_____   _____
_____   _____
_____   _____

Groomsmen's Attire:

_____
_____
_____
_____
_____

Tux Rental Appointments: Time:

_____   _____
_____   _____
_____   _____
_____   _____
_____   _____

Shopping Tips

When shopping for attire for your groom and his attendants, consider the following questions:

■ Based on your Buzz Words (page 14) and Inspiration Board (page 32), how formal will the men's attire be?

_____

■ Does a tuxedo or a suit fit your groom's personality better?

_____

■ Will your groom be styled differently from his groomsmen?

_____

■ Does your groom prefer a more luxurious and tailored look, or is he more concerned with affordability?

_____

■ Are you planning to buy or rent your formalwear?

_____

■ How will the formalwear be ordered? Do the guys need to be measured in person, or will they be able to send their measurements to the store?

_____

■ When will the formalwear be tailored?

_____

■ What is the purchase/rental return policy?

_____

■ Will you purchase accessories for the men, or are accessories part of a rental package? The groom may want to give his groomsmen a particular tie or cufflinks to personalize the guys' attire.

_____

■ Who is paying?

_____

 *Southern touch*

For warm-weather weddings, purchase or rent a "backup shirt" for the men. This way, humidity and perspiration will not make the guys look less than their best in photos. Plus, the attendants will thank you, as no one likes to be uncomfortable while in the spotlight.

For Kids and Kids at Heart

Don't forget about children and parents. Consider asking these key people to dress in styles, colors, and fabrics that complement the overall look of the bridal party. Your family photos will look wonderful!

Planning the Ceremony

This is what your wedding day is all about. The most important part of your day will be walking down the aisle to make the change from "single" to "married." As fun as it is to plan the details of your dress and the reception, it is equally important to spend time planning and personalizing your ceremony. And make sure to include your fiancé in the process.

Keep in mind that planning a ceremony in a place of worship can be very different from planning one outside of a religious venue. Make sure you have first established a venue that is right for the two of you.

Types of Ceremonies

Religious ceremony in a house of worship

If you are marrying in a church or synagogue, the most important things to consider are the guidelines of the location. Every religion and house of worship within has varying rules, processes, and instructions that you will be expected to follow with the guidance of the clergyperson who will marry you.

In many cases, the marrying couple is expected to be practicing members within the religion and/or house of worship. And you may be required to attend services and even pre-wedding courses. Be sure to inquire about a handbook on policies that you can carefully review as you start making your ceremony plans.

When you meet with your officiant to start discussing the ceremony, be sure to find out what his or her service style will be like and how much input the two of you will have with personalizing the service.

Questions to consider asking for planning a religious ceremony:

☐ *How long do ceremonies typically last?*

_____

_____

☐ *Will there be a sermon or speech?*

_____

_____

☐ *Are you able to write your own vows?*

_____

_____

☐ *Can you select readings?*

_____

_____

☐ *Do you need to attend any prenuptial classes or counseling courses?*

_____

_____

☐ *Do you need to adhere to policies about the way you dress (e.g., shoulders must be covered, etc.)?*

_____

_____

☐ *When will you have the wedding rehearsal?*

_____

_____

details, details, details

Ceremony fees

If you are getting married in a house of worship, there might be a wedding service fee. Churches often do not charge fees to current members, but a donation to the clergyperson or church is appreciated to show your gratitude.

Suggested amounts:

Religious officiant: The contribution amount is typically $100 - $400.

Hired officiant: Fees typically start at $250 for the wedding day plus travel expenses. The officiant may charge an additional amount to attend the wedding rehearsal practice.

Civil ceremony officiant: Fees vary and depend on whether the officiant will be onsite at city hall or with you offsite at a venue.

Friend performing the ceremony: Typically, a personal gift is appropriate rather than a cash payment.

Others: Don't forget to show your gratitude to church musicians, altar assistants, and anyone else who has worked on your wedding ceremony.

☐ *Are there cantors, musicians, etc., whom you need to book through the house of worship, or can you bring them in from outside?*

_____

_____

☐ *What are the rules for photographers and videographers on the day of the wedding?*

_____

_____

☐ *Who will take care of filling out and mailing back your marriage license following the ceremony?*

_____

_____

Civil ceremony

A civil ceremony is a nonreligious ceremony typically performed by a government official, such as a judge or justice of the peace or even a friend who has been approved and registered to perform a wedding ceremony. A civil ceremony can be just as poignant as a religious ceremony, and the length, formality, and style are dependent on the couple.

Be sure to carefully research what process, forms, and fees are required, since laws vary in states and counties.

_____

_____

Interfaith ceremony

It is very common today that couples getting married are of different religious backgrounds. In some cases, a house of worship will allow dual officiants, one to represent each religion, to preside over the ceremony together. It is also an option to have two separate ceremonies to honor the traditions of each religion. In this case, only one ceremony will be represented on the official wedding certificate and marriage license.

Components of the Ceremony

The readings and readers

If you have a special friend or family member you would like to include in the ceremony, having that person read is a wonderful way to acknowledge his or her importance. To figure out what you would like to be read, begin by talking with your partner about what makes your relationship unique. Think about how you met, how far you've come, what you want for your future, what you believe in, and how in love you are. Imagine your ceremony setting and how your favorite poetry, novels, scripture, or inspiring words will sound being read aloud by a dear friend or recited by the two of you.

If you are to be married in a church, discuss the process of selecting readings with your officiant. He or she will offer guidance and possibly a list of suggested scripture readings for you to select from. As it is not always possible to customize each suggested reading to your tastes, ask your officiant to make it a point to personalize his or her address so it best represents the two of you to your guests.

Tips for selecting readings and readers:

- ☐ Take time selecting your readings. Is it a good idea to practice reciting the potential options with your partner to see how each one sounds? Are the words hard to follow? Is the length too long?

- ☐ Pair each of your selected readings with a specific person. When you ask that person to be a reader, acknowledge that he or she is an important person in your lives.

- ☐ Don't pressure friends to read if they are concerned about public speaking. There are plenty of other important roles that will need an honored guest.

- ☐ Give each reader plenty of time to prepare and practice. Offer guidance on what to expect, what to wear, etc.

- ☐ Consider acknowledging your readers in your ceremony program and offering an explanation of why their address is important to the two of you.

Music, hymns, and songs

Just as a musical score heightens the senses during a movie or theatrical performance, it will do the same for your wedding. Music helps set the scene, provides thoughtful pauses, and offers subtle cues to keep the occasion moving along.

You may want to hire a pianist, organist, soloist, or string quartet. Perhaps you have a family member or good friend who will offer you the gift of his or her talent—be it with touching vocals or scene-setting music. And be sure to discuss with your partner whether you will include music before and/or during your ceremony.

- Consider having prelude music playing softly in the background as your guests arrive.

- Ask if there are limitations on what types of songs may be performed. If you will be married in a house of worship, it is in good taste that music be of a religious nature.

- If you are requesting specific arrangements or non-traditional songs, allow your music vendors plenty of time to learn each piece.

Music is most commonly used to enhance the following parts of a ceremony:

- Prelude: _____
- Seating of the Family: _____
- Procession of the Bridal Party: _____
- Bridal Processional: _____
- Interlude: _____
- Recessional: _____

details, details, details

Popular ceremony selections:

"Adagio"
Felix Mendelssohn

"Air on the G String"
Johann S. Bach

"Bridal Chorus"
Richard Wagner

"Canon in D"
Johann Pachelbel

"Hallelujah Chorus"
George F. Handel

"Hornpipe" George F. Handel

"Joyful, Joyful, We Adore Thee" traditional hymn

"Ode to Joy"
Ludwig van Beethoven

"Sheep May Safely Graze"
Johann S. Bach

"Simple Gifts"
Joseph Brackett

"Spring" Antonio Vivaldi

"The Arrival of the Queen of Sheba" George F. Handel

"Trumpet Voluntary"
Jeremiah Clarke

"Wedding March"
Wolfgang Amadeus Mozart

"Water Music"
George F. Handel

Be sure to check out iTunes for samples of songs. Create a playlist of pieces that you enjoy and then share it with potential vendors or with the music director from the church.

Southern touch

A timeless detail and way to personalize the ceremony is to engrave a sentiment inside your partner's ring. Consider a few words from a reading, your wedding date, or ceremony location. After the wedding is over, take a moment to reveal your secret message to your spouse.

The vows

Your wedding vows may be the most profound words that you and your future spouse will ever exchange. Therefore, it's important to give them a lot of thought. Think about what the words mean for you as a couple.

If you are exchanging traditional vows:

- **Embrace the beauty of the timeless words.** Short of addressing your partner when speaking your vows, there is little that you may want or be allowed to personalize. Instead, invest your creativity in personalizing the program. Perhaps indicate why you have chosen to recite traditional vows of faith and love.

- **Decide as a couple if you will memorize your vows.** You may decide that although your officiant is important, having that person a bit more removed from the vow exchange will keep the focus on the two of you. If you go this route, you might want to ask your officiant to be "standing by" just in case you are overcome with emotion and forget your lines.

If you feel more comfortable writing your own vows:

You may discover that traditional vows fail to adequately express your love and commitment to each other. If so, alter them, or better yet, compose your own.

- **Brainstorm** about the kind of commitment you intend to make.

- **Write down words that describe your relationship,** and ask your partner to do the same. Use these words as a "verbal map" to guide you as you put your thoughts on paper.

- **Decide if you will read or memorize your vows.** Be mindful of the length of your vows when making your decision.

- **If you will not be writing your vows together** or sharing your vows before the ceremony, set some writing guidelines to ensure consistency (like writing style, length, etc.).

A nice ring to it...

What should you do with the rings during the ceremony? Most brides and grooms offer the rings to the best man to hold until the officiant asks for them. If you will be having a child serve as the ring bearer, it is a good idea to have him carry a pretty ring pillow and leave the actual rings in the hands of your most honored groomsman.

Southern touch

Something old, something new, something borrowed, and something blue!

This wedding tradition dates back to the Victorian era and symbolizes continuity with the bride's past, optimism for her life ahead, and good fortune and love in her married life. It can be fun to take part in this tradition, and you can make it Southern by incorporating things like family heirlooms, lockets, handkerchiefs, or even a piece of lace from your mother or grandmother's veil or gown for something "old" or "borrowed." Ask your gown seamstress to sew a tag into your dress with your wedding date in blue thread to cover the something "new" and "blue."

Wedding Traditions

Every religion and culture has certain customs and traditions that are often embraced by couples as part of their ceremony. Doing so is a nice way to incorporate heritages. You may want to also embrace a new ritual to add a personal touch to the day.

Blessing of rings: In some cultures, instead of having the officiant "bless" the rings, the rings are passed around to guests for their blessings before they are worn by the couple.

Chuppah: This is a wedding canopy under which the couple is married. In the Jewish faith, it signifies the couple's new home together. A prayer shawl, or tallit, is also held over the couple by four family members or friends.

Ketubah: This is a Jewish prenuptial agreement signed in a ceremony (prior to the wedding ceremony) by the bride, groom, and two witnesses. It is later read by the rabbi under the chuppah during the service.

Parent recognition: This is often done with a flower boutonniere or corsage to represent parents and grandparents of the bride and groom. In Jewish tradition, the groom and bride are escorted down the aisle by their parents.

Tying the knot: The couple's hands are loosely tied together by a sash or cord to symbolize the union of marriage.

Unity candle: This involves two taper candles with a large pillar candle (called the "unity candle") in the center. At the beginning of the wedding ceremony, a representative from each family (usually the mothers of the bride and groom) light the two taper candles. Later in the ceremony, following the vows, the bride and groom use the two taper candles to light the large pillar "unity candle" together.

Unveiling and veiling of the bride: Traditionally, the bride is unveiled by her father after he escorts her down the aisle and "gives her away." In Jewish tradition, there is often a ceremony called a Badeken that is held just before the wedding. At this time, the groom veils the bride.

Wedding rings: The rings represent the covenant of marriage between partners. The circle of the ring symbolizes the couple's love that knows no beginning and no end.

Ceremony Placement

Below and on the next two pages are traditional guidelines for seating arrangements, procession, standing formation, and recession. Depending on where you are getting married, some arrangements might need to be modified.

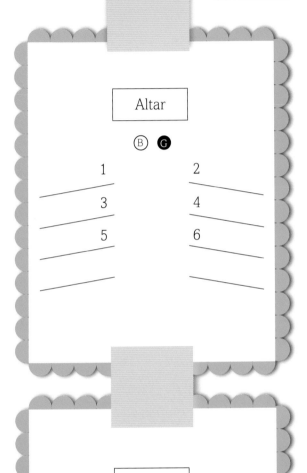

Seating at a Christian Ceremony

1. Bride's Parents
2. Groom's Parents
3. Bride's Grandparents and Siblings
4. Groom's Grandparents and Siblings
5. Bride's Special Guests
6. Groom's Special Guests

Seating at a Jewish Ceremony

1. Groom's Grandparents and Siblings
2. Bride's Grandparents and Siblings
3. Groom's Special Guests
4. Bride's Special Guests

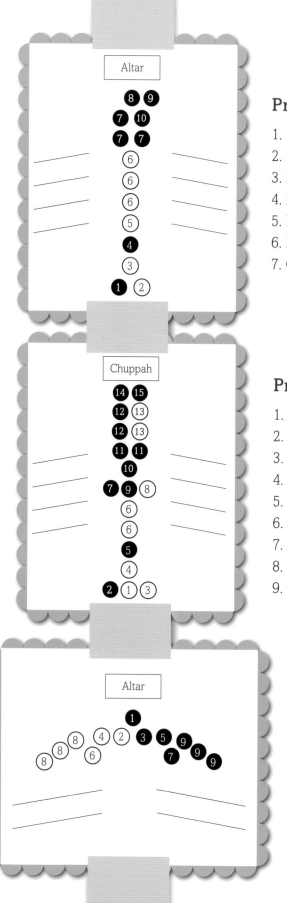

Procession at a Christian Ceremony

1. Bride's Father
2. Bride
3. Flower Girl
4. Ring Bearer
5. Honor Attendant
6. Bridesmaid
7. Groomsman
8. Officiant
9. Groom
10. Best Man

Procession at a Jewish Ceremony

1. Bride
2. Bride's Father
3. Bride's Mother
4. Flower Girl
5. Ring Bearer
6. Bridesmaid
7. Groom's Father
8. Groom's Mother
9. Groom
10. Best Man
11. Groomsman
12. Bride's/Groom's Grandfather
13. Bride's/Groom's Grandmother
14. Rabbi
15. Cantor

Standing Formation for a Christian Ceremony

1. Officiant
2. Bride
3. Groom
4. Honor Attendant
5. Best Man
6. Flower Girl
7. Ring Bearer
8. Bridesmaid
9. Groomsman

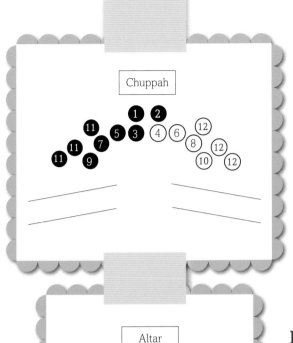

Standing Formation for a Jewish Ceremony

1. Rabbi
2. Cantor
3. Groom
4. Bride
5. Best Man
6. Honor Attendant
7. Groom's Parents
8. Bride's Parents
9. Ring Bearer
10. Flower Girl
11. Groomsman
12. Bridesmaid

Recession at a Christian Ceremony

1. Bride
2. Groom
3. Flower Girl
4. Ring Bearer
5. Honor Attendant
6. Best Man
7. Bridesmaid
8. Groomsman

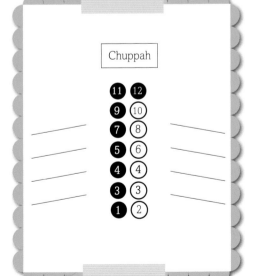

Recession at a Jewish Ceremony

1. Groom
2. Bride
3. Bride's Parents
4. Groom's Parents
5. Ring Bearer
6. Flower Girl
7. Best Man
8. Honor Attendant
9. Groomsman
10. Bridesmaid
11. Rabbi
12. Cantor

The Pronouncement

Congratulations! This is the moment you are introduced as a married couple to your family and friends for the first time. Take a minute to share a kiss and turn to your congregation. Be sure to pause briefly before you begin your walk back down the aisle, giving your photographer a few seconds to snap the perfect picture. You may want to plan to take a few minutes alone at this point and enjoy your first moments as husband and wife.

The Receiving Line

Some couples choose to honor the tradition of a receiving line. If you have more than 50 guests at your wedding, etiquette suggests that a receiving line is the right thing to do. A receiving line may be formed immediately after the ceremony (or sometimes during the cocktail hour). This allows guests the opportunity to offer their congratulations (or in some cases introduce themselves) to the newlyweds and each honored guest. Typically, the bride's parents will "host" the receiving line and be joined by the newlyweds, maid of honor, best man, and the groom's parents. If you are planning to hold a receiving line, let these key people know in advance.

words of wisdom: Don't forget to account for the receiving line in your wedding day agenda. As wonderful as they are, they can certainly take quite a bit of time to complete.

Decor Details

Decorations can play a significant part in the beauty and meaning of the ceremony. Decide if you want to decorate your ceremony location and how much you are willing to invest. Many ceremony locations are selected for the simple reason that they are beautiful enough already and need very little adornment. Others may need a little enhancement. Before you sit down with your Buzz Words and Four Ss, ask the representative from your location if decorations are allowed. Many churches and religious buildings have a set of suggested guidelines outlining how the venue should be decorated.

If you are planning to reserve seats for honored guests, consider designating several seats in the front rows on either side of the aisle. A pretty floral adornment, a "Reserved" card, or a classic ribbon swag are some easy ideas to combine form and function when it comes to politely holding these seats.

words of wisdom: If you are married in a church or other house of worship, consider leaving your floral arrangements for the parish to enjoy. It is a small but greatly enjoyed way to say thank you!

Wedding Program

Not only can programs continue the mood set by your invitations, but they can also help guests follow along with your ceremony. There are many styles of programs, from the very simple to the overly notated. Regardless of what style you choose, be sure to use the program as a platform for personalizing your ceremony. As guests read along in their programs, it helps them to feel as much a part of your day as your honored attendants. Approach the creation of your program with thought, assuming that your guests will hold onto it as a keepsake of your union. Use your Buzz Words to guide the printed narration of the ceremony. As you prepare your text for the stationer, consider including the following elements.

What to include:

- Begin with the basics of your names, ceremony location, and the date.

- Consider including a note from you and your partner thanking your guests for traveling to be with you on your special day.

- Honor your attendants, readers, vocalists, greeters, ushers, and other participants by listing their names. You may opt to go a step further and note how you know them and why they are special to you.

- Provide a bit of history and explanation on faith-specific customs or family traditions that will be represented during the service. This will make guests who are witnessing these meaningful acts feel welcome and at ease.

- Include music selections and readings, noting where verbal responses from guests are requested.

- At the end of the program, it is nice to print how you would like to be recognized as a couple (to indicate if there are to be any name changes) and your home address.

At Home

Mr. and Mrs. Joshua Paul

2010 Capitol Hill Circle, Northwest

Washington, D.C. 20001

Wedding Ceremony Location Checklist

Having an outside ceremony can be very different from having an inside ceremony. Here are considerations to make for each:

Inside ceremonies

- [ ] What time will the venue be available before the wedding starts?
- [ ] Is there a separate holding area for both the bride and groom and their respective bridal parties?
- [ ] Does the "bridal room" have a mirror and access to a restroom?
- [ ] What are the policies on floral decor?
- [ ] For churches, do you have to leave any altar flower arrangements for the church post-ceremony?
- [ ] Are you allowed to hang flowers or decor on pews?
- [ ] Are you permitted to use an aisle runner and how will it be secured?
- [ ] Where will musicians be located and will they have a line of sight to the aisle?
- [ ] Does the venue allow for photography and videography?
- [ ] Are guests permitted to take pictures?
- [ ] Are there sections of seating that ushers should avoid?
- [ ] Where will the bridal party line up and process from?
- [ ] Are there any policies that must be listed in the program to guests (*e.g.*, no photography permitted, all men must wear a yarmulke, etc.).

Outside ceremonies

- [ ] What time will the venue be available before the wedding starts?
- [ ] Is there a separate holding area for both the bride and groom and their respective bridal parties?
- [ ] Does the "bridal room" have a mirror and access to a restroom?
- [ ] Can you decorate the aisle with anything (*e.g.*, petals, etc.)?
- [ ] How is seating typically arranged?
- [ ] Think about your guests' comfort. Will the sun be setting in front or behind guests? Will it be warm? Should you offer water or fans? Will it be chilly?
- [ ] Will you have microphone(s) and speakers to project the officiant, bride/groom and readers? Where will power come from to run the sound?
- [ ] Do you need to provide a lectern stand for the officiant?
- [ ] Do you need a table for displaying a unity candle or other accessories like a ketubah?
- [ ] Where will musicians be located, and will they have a line of sight to the aisle?
- [ ] Where will the bridal party line up and process from?
- [ ] What will be the rain plan for the ceremony?

make it yours

On the day of the wedding, put a special friend in charge of making sure the programs, reserved signs, and accessories such as unity candles make it to the church on time. Be sure readers have copies of their readings with them and that a copy of the readings is also given to the officiant. Ushers should be instructed on seating specifications, such as whether there is a specific side for the bride or groom and which front seats are reserved for the family and bridal party.

words of wisdom: If you are having an outdoor wedding, especially on the beach, you might need to be flexible about which side you stand on depending on the direction of the wind. You don't want your hair or veil blowing into your face during the ceremony.

Marriage License

The specifications for obtaining a marriage license vary among states. A good place to start is to research your state's guidelines, including what timeframe prior to the wedding you must apply for the license. Typically you must apply at least 30 days before the wedding date, and both parties must appear in person with valid identification.

After the marriage ceremony, both spouses and the officiant sign the marriage license (some states also require a witness). The officiant or couple then files for a certified copy of the marriage license and a marriage certificate with the appropriate authority. Some states also have requirements that a license be filed within a certain time after its issuance, typically 30 or 60 days, following which a new license must be obtained.

Capture the Memories

At the end of your wedding day, you'll hang up your dress and put away your dancing shoes. Your guests will travel home, your bouquet will lose its luster, and your cake topper will settle in for the year in the freezer. You'll be left with dreamy memories of the happiest day of your life. So perhaps the most important decision you'll make in your planning process is selecting the person who will capture those memories on camera. The preservation of your wedding will become the responsibility of the photographer and videographer whom you entrust to visually document the story of your day so you may share it with generations to come.

Finding the right "fit" with these vendors is the key to great wedding memories. You will want to connect with their personalities, trust in their abilities and suggestions, and respect their individuality and talent.

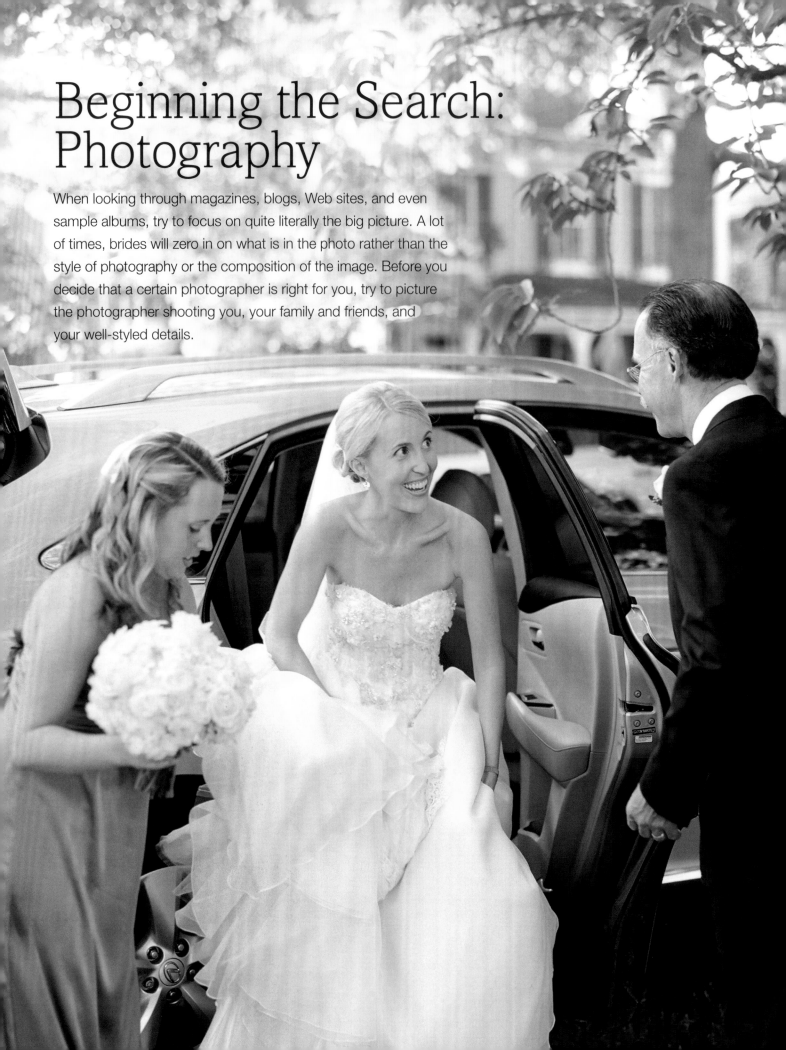

Beginning the Search: Photography

When looking through magazines, blogs, Web sites, and even sample albums, try to focus on quite literally the big picture. A lot of times, brides will zero in on what is in the photo rather than the style of photography or the composition of the image. Before you decide that a certain photographer is right for you, try to picture the photographer shooting you, your family and friends, and your well-styled details.

Types of Wedding Photography: Defining Your Style

If you don't know what you are looking for in wedding photography, start by reviewing your Four Ss and Buzz Words (pages 13 and 14) and searching for a photographer whose style will enhance your vision. A rustic farm wedding may be better matched with a photographer who focuses on outdoor weddings and uses lots of natural light, whereas a city wedding in a modern museum may be better captured by a digital photographer with a stylized eye. Generally speaking, there are two major categories that encompass wedding photography: editorial/fine art and photojournalism.

Editorial/Fine art

Editorial or fine art photography is an interactive experience between the bride, groom, and photographer. A fine art photographer works with the couple to compose the image, offering direction and suggestions for what will make the photo look its best. Fine art photography may range in style from traditional to a bit more modern and will offer well-composed photographs that are aesthetically pleasing and technically excellent.

Photojournalism

Photojournalism might best be described as a "reporting" style of photography. The photographer tends to take a more observatory approach in shooting, capturing moments as they unfold. The lasting images will be emotional, matter-of-fact, and timeless.

Establishing Expectations

When it comes to working with your photographer, the feeling between the two of you should be "picture perfect." You will want to be absolutely sure you are both on the same page and that you are clearly communicating your expectations. At the same time, it is important that you listen and respect the photographer's advice to you.

Your photographer will have a technical knowledge that he or she has acquired through years of experience with shooting, and this becomes extremely important to consider for your wedding day. It is wise to take the photographer's advice on the best locations for taking group photos and at what time of day you will get the best results for outside pictures. A professional photographer will have your best interests in mind—and you should too.

Interviewing and Selecting Your Photographer

Just like other forms of artistic expression, photography is open to interpretation. As you evaluate sample images and speak with different photographers, remember that each artist takes a different approach to his or her work. For some, it is transactional—they offer a service, you pay a fee, and a final product is delivered. For other photographers, they value their work as almost transcendental—they take on a limited number of "perfect fit" clients and bond with them throughout the process.

words of wisdom: If you are having an outside wedding ceremony and/or reception, be sure to check what the local sunset times will be and plan accordingly for photos. Your photographer will have a very difficult job capturing good images if there is not adequate light available.

Consider the photographer a good fit for you when you can positively answer the following questions:

Questions	Photographer Name:	Photographer Name:	Photographer Name:
Do you feel comfortable with the photographer's personality?			
Is his or her approach to shooting the day a method that you feel is a good fit for you and your family?			
Do you completely understand the investment and what deliverables you receive?			
Did you get positive feedback from references?			
Is the photographer excited and understanding of your Buzz Words and Four Ss?			

When speaking or meeting with photographers, take time to ask questions. To get the conversation started, here are few things to consider:

Questions	Photographer Name:	Photographer Name:	Photographer Name:
How long has the photographer been shooting weddings?			
Is this his or her full-time job, or does the photographer do weddings on the side?			
What is the wedding day like for the photographer? When does he or she arrive/leave?			
What is the approach taken with shooting? Will the photographer offer advice and guidance or just let events and moments unfold?			
Will the photographer bring an assistant? Is the assistant actually shooting or serving more as the "right hand" to the photographer?			
What are you allowed to do with the photos? What is the photographer allowed to do with the photos?			
Ask to see the pictures from a recent wedding from start to finish.			
Ask to see a sample album.			

Pricing

A great photographer is a priceless investment when it comes to preserving your memories. This investment should be put near the top of the wedding-budget priority list, because experience and quality come with a price tag. When deciding how much to invest, think about your Four Ss (page 13) and Buzz Words (page 14).

Pricing varies across the country, and each photographer sets his or her own rules. When speaking with potential photographers, ask how they charge. Most offer packages with a selected number of hours included or a flat rate for a day of unlimited coverage.

Use the chart below to compare your top three favorite photographers:

Questions to consider	Photographer Name:	Photographer Name:	Photographer Name:
Price			
Number of Hours			
Second Shooter			
Album Included			
Travel Fees			
Standout feature(s)			

Engagement Session

Engagement pictures are a great way to get to know your photographer and to practice taking pictures before you are in your wedding dress. An engagement session is usually a more informal experience. Most modern-day engagement sessions involve a relaxed setting that showcases the couple doing something they enjoy. The environment of these shoots is usually simple and classic but may be more staged and styled, depending on the personality of the couple and photographer. Regardless of which direction you choose, inspiration for engagement sessions is everywhere!

When are you planning to get ready? *Most people do not want to be photographed without having hair and makeup in place first.*

_____
_____
_____
_____
_____
_____

When will the dancing portion of the event be in full swing? *If you are not planning a send-off, 30 minutes of high-energy dancing should be plenty of time to give you the fun "party" images you might be looking for.*

_____
_____
_____
_____
_____

Photography and Your Wedding Agenda

Two months prior to the wedding, establish a wedding day agenda that will note all of the day's milestones and the times and locations at which these events will occur. It is critical to not only provide your photographer with this schedule but also to get his or her input early on regarding what you have planned.

As you build your agenda with photography in mind, be sure to carefully understand what your photography package includes for the wedding day. It is helpful to work backward through the day to determine what the photographer's arrival and departure times should be. For example, you may want 10 hours of photography as well as a photographer who stays until the end of the festivities. So if your wedding day ends at 11 p.m., coverage will start at 1 p.m. Think about what you will be doing at 1 p.m. Do you want the photographer to arrive at your hotel suite after hair and makeup but before you step into your dress? Are you comfortable having a photographer in your presence when you are getting dressed? What time will your ceremony begin?

You will also want to discuss key moments during the day that the photographer will be responsible for directing, such as a "first look," family photos, and any other special moments that will need time on the schedule. Discuss not only the amount of time you will need to set aside for these events but also where they will take place. Remember to consider inclement weather options as well.

Your Photographer's Needs

Remember to discuss logistical details with your photographer, such as how he or she will get around if your wedding ceremony and reception are in different locations. Consider inviting your photographer to ride along in the car with you. Moments in a car ride, before the ceremony with your parents and after the ceremony with your new husband, are great material for your photographer to capture.

Be sure to pay attention to any requirements your photographer has included in the contract. Most photographers will require a vendor meal and will break to eat when the bride and groom sit down to eat (since nobody wants photos of themselves eating!). Note on your wedding agenda when the photographer will be eating and do not schedule any events, such as toasts, to take place during that time.

Most important of all, do not try to overly manage or stifle your photographer's creative process. After all, you hired the photographer because you loved his or her work, and you want the same results from your day!

words of wisdom: Tell your caterer during the planning process that you expect the photographer to be fed when the two of you are eating. Sometimes caterers will want to feed guests first and vendors last, but this could cause your photographer to miss an important moment.

Photography Notes

- Photographer Start Time:

_____

_____

- Photographer End Time:

_____

_____

- Special Moments/Time:

_____

_____

First Look

A growing trend in weddings is the bride and groom wanting to see each other prior to the ceremony in order to share an intimate moment together and to capture the emotions of seeing each other for the first time on the big day.

Pros:

- The two of you are able to relish a bit of privacy seeing each other for the first time and sharing those feelings together.

- Your photographer will be able to capture pictures of you together and won't have to steal you away during cocktail hour or the reception to get pictures of the most important group—the two of you!

- Most couples feel a bit more relaxed and less nervous after seeing each other.

Cons:

- It goes a bit against tradition.

- If you have been waiting your whole life for your husband-to-be to see you for the first time when you are walking down the aisle, this might not be the right option for you.

The decision to look, or not to look, is a very personal one and should be carefully considered by the two of you according to what makes sense in the big picture of the day's schedule.

details, details, details

**Smile!
Wedding Day Tips:**

Most brides and grooms are a bit nervous and self-conscious about being in the spotlight on the big day, and it can sometimes feel a bit unnatural to have a camera capturing your every move. Follow these tips to look your best:

❊ Relax! Don't try to look for the camera on your big day—the camera will find you. Some of the best pictures will be of you enjoying the day while unaware you are even being captured on film.

❊ For portrait shots, be sure to look directly at the camera for the best results.

❊ Straighten up! Use good posture and stand straight—slouching does not look pretty, even in a gorgeous wedding dress.

❊ Leave your gum at home! The no-chewing rule applies to the entire bridal party.

❊ Have your maid of honor carry your lip gloss for you so you can easily touch up and remain fresh for photos.

Group Photo Tips:

Family photos often follow the ceremony, which allows only a small amount of time for these. Set your photographer up for success in advance by doing the following things:

❋ Be sure that anyone you want to include in family photos is aware of when these photos will take place and where to gather.

❋ Ask a reliable family member to assist in corralling any stragglers who might forget they are needed for photos.

❋ Provide the photographer with any distinguishable characteristics of family members since he or she will not know what "Grandma" or "cousin Erica" looks like.

Must-have Photo List

The photos you want taken on your wedding day might not be obvious to your photographer. So when you discuss your wedding day agenda with your photographer, you will also want to provide a list of photos that you want captured. This list will be a combination of groups of family, bridal party members, and friends. If you have a great aunt who is extremely dear to you and you want to make certain you get a photo with her, you need to include that on your list. Your photographer cannot be faulted for not capturing this if you have not included such directions.

It is important to speak with your photographer about a shooting schedule for the wedding day. Allow your photographer to help create the schedule so you will maximize his or her time and talent. The following worksheet will help you to plan the group photos you would like to take.

Wedding Photography Vocabulary

☐ **Digital photography:** Pictures are captured digitally. This is the preferred method of most photographers.

☐ **Disc of images:** A DVD (or sometimes CD) of all of the wedding images the photographer has available for you.

☐ **Film photography:** Pictures are captured using film and must be sent to a lab to be processed and developed.

☐ **High and low resolution:** Refers to the image resolution of the picture based on size and pixels. High-resolution photos are generally needed for printing, and low-resolution images are better for viewing on computers.

☐ **Slideshow:** Your photographer will select his or her favorite images from the wedding and put them into a presentation, often set to music. The slideshow is generally online with the viewing gallery.

☐ **Viewing or "proofing" gallery:** An online private gallery that will allow you, your family, and your friends to view all of the finished images. Often these galleries will also allow friends and family to directly purchase photos themselves.

Must-have Photo List Worksheet

Important photos

- ☐ Bride and groom together
- ☐ All family gathered (both sets of parents, all siblings on both sides, etc.)
- ☐ Bride and groom with groom's parents and siblings
- ☐ Bride and groom with groom's parents
- ☐ Bride and groom with bride's parents and siblings
- ☐ Bride and groom with bride's parents
- ☐ Bride and groom with groom's grandparents
- ☐ Bride and groom with bride's grandparents
- ☐ Bride with her parents
- ☐ Groom with his parents
- ☐ Bride and groom with bride's siblings
- ☐ Bride and groom with groom's siblings
- ☐ Bride and groom with any child attendants
- ☐ Bride alone
- ☐ Groom alone

Bridal Party

- ☐ Entire bridal party
- ☐ Bride with bridesmaids
- ☐ Groom with groomsmen
- ☐ Bride with maid of honor
- ☐ Groom with best man
- ☐ _____
- ☐ _____
- ☐ _____
- ☐ _____

Other

- ☐ Dress and accessories
- ☐ Room shots and decor (before guests enter the room)
- ☐ Invitations and other details
- ☐ Cake (before it is cut)
- ☐ Food shots
- ☐ Other wedding details like family photo displays, guest book, etc.
- ☐ _____
- ☐ _____
- ☐ _____
- ☐ _____

Southern touch

Parent albums are a wonderful way to help each family remember your wedding day. These albums are usually smaller versions of the wedding album with a focus on that particular side of the family. If you are planning parent albums, ask each set of parents to use the same checklist process as on the previous page and to note their favorite images. Having them work directly with the photographer will help achieve an album designed to their tastes.

After the Wedding

Your photographer's work is just beginning when your wedding day ends. Film may need to be developed, and thousands of images will be sorted through and edited. Your photographer's contract should outline a timeframe in which you will receive your images. Many photographers will present your pictures in an online gallery so you may share them with your family and friends. It's exciting to look forward to reliving your wedding day when your pictures arrive.

Your Album

Each photographer handles the creative approach to album design a little differently. Some will select their favorite images and present a "rough draft" copy to you for feedback, while others will invite you to work on the design with them. One way to achieve a great album is to offer a little bit of guidance to your photographer by mentioning your favorite photographs that you absolutely "must see" in the finished album. Ask your photographer about the average amount of images that he or she likes to use in albums, and keep that number in mind as you sort through your photographs.

If you did not order an album in your photography package, there are plenty of online resources to help you create your own memory book. Online print houses and self-publishers offer an array of products that can be customized to your needs at affordable prices. This option would be a perfect fit for the bride whose photographer provides only a disc of high-resolution images. Additionally, a nice perk is that many of these sites offer discounts for multiple copies of custom-printed pieces, allowing parents, siblings, and other family members or friends to order their own memory books.

words of wisdom: You want the photographer to give you a final product that spotlights his or her best work. Don't be surprised if one or two pictures taken during the day do not make it to your inbox. Your photographer will not want to show you unflattering faces or relatives with their eyes closed in pictures.

Videography

Many couples not only want the still moments captured but also the sounds and movements of the day so they can watch the festivities for years to come.

When selecting a videographer, there are several styles and options to consider:

- **Documentary:** Footage from the moments of the day are pieced together to tell a story. It often blends interviews with live moments, music, and other techniques.

- **Motion Picture:** Footage is highly edited down to a few minutes that are set to music, with snippets of speaking and sounds of the day spliced in. This style has a cinematic appeal.

- **Super 8:** Uses a vintage Super 8 camera and film. This style is very unique and has a timeless quality and appeal. It is typically edited into a few minutes of footage and set to music because it does not capture sound.

- **Traditional:** Captures the moments as they occur and uses editing on the back end to create a mood with music, fades, and other technical features.

Your videographer will offer package options that include a set amount of hours to cover filming the day, cameras and equipment that will capture the footage, editing options, and a finished product that is typically in the form of an HD DVD or an online link.

Be sure to carefully research and review past work of possible videographers to decide what style is right for you. If you are speaking with a company that has multiple videographers, confirm that you are seeing the work of the individual who will be working on your event. As you chat with and interview videographers, discuss upfront what his or her personal style and approach will be on the wedding day to be sure you are comfortable with it. It is also just as important to discuss what the videographer's editing style will be on the back end, as well as the amount of final, edited footage that will be included in your film. The last thing you want is a distraction during your first dance with an oversize camera and bright lights or tacky effects inserted into your finished product.

Establishing Expectations

Similar to your method of working with your photographer, you will need to understand what your videographer's needs and approach will be on the wedding day.

- Review your wedding agenda with the videographer so that he or she is familiar with the schedule.

- Be sure any needed breaks for a meal are planned. Similar to the photographer, a videographer will most likely want to eat when you are eating since there will be no filming during this time.

- It is also important to discuss how the videographer will interact with your photographer on the wedding day since they will both be trying to capture the same footage. Be sure they are familiar with one another and can effectively coordinate how they will work together, especially in a confined space such as a house of worship. The last thing you want is your photographer and videographer in each other's shots.

- If you have a videographer scheduled for only a select amount of hours, be sure you schedule key events to take place during that time.

Your entire day will be a whirlwind of emotions and moments that you will want to treasure. And with the right research and planning, you will have the visual images that will perfectly preserve the memories forever.

Set Your Style

With the exception of your rehearsal the evening before your big day, nothing will quite make your wedding feel closer than receiving your guests' RSVP cards in the mail. In today's world of e-mail clutter and predominantly online correspondence, guests are sure to pay attention when they find a pristine envelope with their name and address handwritten in beautiful calligraphy in their mailbox. The personal invitation inside will provide plenty of excitement about your upcoming celebration and help prompt invitees to let you know that they plan to attend.

From your save-the-date announcement and/or wedding invitation to mementos for your guests to take home with them and the thank-you notes you will send later, paper goods will play a very important role before, during, and after your wedding. While there is no set etiquette stating that your stationery and other paper products should match, using complementary pieces will help you customize the look and style of your special day and make it uniquely yours.

Branding Your Wedding

Before you choose any paper goods for your wedding, look at the pieces shown on the pages of this planner to see how different design elements were mixed to create a custom look and style—a "brand." Also keep in mind your Four Ss and your Buzz Words (pages 13 and 14), your overall style for your special occasion, and your color and design preferences. You want to weave all the elements of your wedding together to create a memorable event that will make everyone exclaim, "This is so them!"

Subtle repetition of complementary colors, fonts, patterns, graphics, and styling will help make each of your paper goods look like a piece from one all-encompassing design. Here are some detail options to keep in mind.

- **Color Palette:** Repeat complementary colors on all of your printed materials and packaging elements, from your save-the-date announcement and/or wedding invitation to welcome bags, ribbon, and thank-you note cards.

- **Font Style:** Choose a unique typographical element and use it consistently.

- **Icon or Motif:** Choose or create a decorative design or pattern and use it consistently.

- **Monogram:** Interweave or pair two or more letters, such as first initials, to create your personal design and use it consistently.

- **Pattern:** Choose or create a decorative design and use that design consistently.

When designing, selecting, or crafting the paper goods for your wedding, resist having each piece produced with an existing font, color, and styling. Instead, "turn the dial" ever so slightly to create new variations that make the pieces uniquely yours.

Paper Goods You Can Use To Brand Your Wedding:

- Save-the-date announcement
- Invitation suite
- Personalized rubber stamp
- Wedding program
- Escort card
- Place card
- Menu card
- Table number or table name
- Signage
- Packaging and tag for favors
- Cocktail napkin
- Coaster
- Welcome bag components and packaging
- Note card for thank-you notes and other correspondence
- Other wedding-related paper products for the rehearsal dinner, welcome parties, brunch, and other events

Creating Your Wedding Web Site

Prior to sending out your official invitation or even your save-the-date announcement, establish your wedding Web site to make it easy to provide guests with detailed information about your wedding ceremony and reception, other related weekend events, and travel information and links so they can plan their trip with ease.

Be sure to include the colors, fonts, patterns, graphics, and styling you are using to brand your wedding in your Web site design. That will help make it look like an integral part of your special occasion.

Here are some suggestions for what to include and consider when building your wedding Web site.

- Include a picture of the two of you since not all guests will have met you both.

- Provide specific information about both the ceremony and reception locations, addresses, and start times. Include links to the venues, if they are available.

- Include the names, phone numbers, and links to hotels where you have made arrangements for your guests to stay. Be sure to note any special room rates, codes, and deadlines for reserving rooms at the group rate.

- Post any logistical details, including whether transportation or valet parking will be provided for guests before and after your wedding ceremony and reception.

- If you are having a destination wedding, it is extremely important to give guests as much information as possible about airports, transportation, favorite restaurants, sightseeing spots, and other details. Don't assume your guests will research this information on their own—they will appreciate your help in making their travel and accommodation planning effortless.

- Include information on locations and itineraries for any other wedding-related events.

- Include links to your wedding registries. It's a subtle way to let guests know where to buy gifts.

Just for fun, include casual pictures of the two of you, the story of how you met, and when and where you became engaged.

Password-protect your Web site for privacy.

Remember to include your wedding Web site address and password on your save-the-date announcement and/or on a wedding invitation insert.

Working with a Stationer

A stationer, a company that sells stationery, has employees who can guide you in designing and ordering your invitation suite. Stationers typically offer the following options.

■ **Web Sites:** Companies that offer wedding invitations online usually allow you to choose from pre-designed templates and customize certain options, such as text, motifs, and colors.

■ **In Store:** Stationery stores often carry invitation suites from a number of designers. You can browse each designer's album to see samples of his or her work and the design templates offered. A store employee can guide you in selecting a design that suits your preferred style and budget.

■ **Custom:** Many stationers work with designers who can create a customized invitation, which is a great route to go if you want to have a wedding that is uniquely you.

Where you order your invitations will dictate how much time you need to allow between placing your order and receiving the printed paper goods. Typically you want to start shopping for your save-the-date announcement and invitations seven to nine months prior to your wedding. Custom designers require more time because they start from scratch and often schedule their jobs in advance—so be sure to allow plenty of time to get on their calendars.

Your stationer will tell you about options for available paper (including sizes, weights, and colors), fonts, and printing methods based on the design you select and your budget. After you settle on a design and provide the text, the stationer will give you a proof of the invitation pieces for your review. Be sure to ask the stationer how many proofs you will be allowed and if there is a charge for revisions you make to the design or text.

Sending a Save-the-Date Announcement

Your save-the-date announcement will give your guests basic information about your upcoming wedding so they can mark the date on their calendars and start planning to attend. Mail these announcements to guests you intend to invite to your wedding at least five to six months prior to your wedding date. If you are having a destination wedding or if you are inviting a large number of guests from out of town, be sure to give them plenty of notice so they can make travel plans.

Here are some suggestions for information to include on your save-the-date announcement:

☐ Bride's and groom's first and last names _____
_____

☐ Wedding date _____
_____

☐ Wedding location _____
_____

☐ Wedding Web site address and password _____
_____

☐ A note with "invitation to follow" so your guests know to look for it in the mail _____
_____

☐ Other special information _____
_____
_____
_____
_____

Selecting Your Invitation Suite

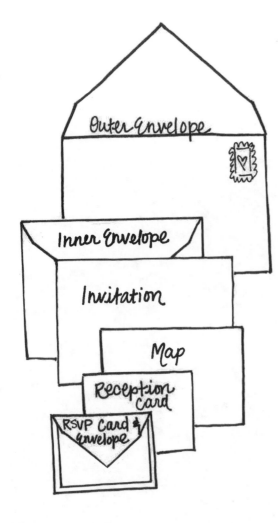

Your wedding invitation is your official notice to guests that their presence is requested at your celebration. Mail your invitations at least eight weeks prior to your wedding date, and give your guests at least four weeks to respond before the RSVP due date.

A wedding invitation suite typically includes the following items:

■ **An outer mailing envelope:** The outer envelope protects the invitation and contains the guest's address, the return address, and the stamp(s).

■ **An inner envelope:** A more formal invitation will include this, but it is not necessary. You may want to omit it to save money.

■ **The wedding invitation:** A typical invitation includes the following lines of information:

☐ **The names of the people hosting the wedding or issuing the invitation:** Typically the parents of the bride host the wedding, but if the groom's parents are co-hosting it, their names are included following the groom's name. If the bride and groom are hosting the wedding, it might read, "Together with their families."

☐ **Request for presence:** Typically a phrase such as "request the honor of your presence" is used.

☐ **Bride's and groom's full names:** The bride's name is listed first, followed by the groom's name.

☐ **Date and time:** Typically the date and time are spelled out on more formal invitations.

words of wisdom:
Before you mail any invitations to your guests, be sure to test-mail one to yourself to make sure you have used the correct amount of postage and to see how the invitation envelope handles in the mail.

☐ **Ceremony location:** Often the name of the house of worship or nonreligious venue is used, and the city and state are listed without an address; for example, Saint John's Church, Washington, District of Columbia. Reception: If the wedding ceremony and reception are in the same location, they can be listed on a single invitation. If they are in different locations, a separate reception card should be included.

☐ **Dress code:** If applicable, the dress code, such as "black tie required," can either be specified in the lower right corner of the invitation or on the reception card insert (see below).

■ **Reception card insert:** If the reception is not being held in the same location as the wedding ceremony, include a reception card giving the name and address of the location, as well as the start time if it will not be starting "immediately following" the ceremony.

■ **Map insert:** This helpful addition gives guests a visual image of the location of hotels, the wedding venues, and other events. It should include specific names and addresses.

■ **Additional inserts:** Often additional information, such as hotel and travel details, is included on inserts. Since inserts require additional paper and printing costs, consider directing guests to your wedding Web site for more information.

■ **RSVP card and envelope:** Guests will complete the RSVP card and return it to you in the envelope. In addition to asking guests to indicate whether they will attend the reception, the RSVP card can also include their meal request, if there is a choice. As a courtesy to your guests, be sure to include postage on the RSVP return envelope.

details, details, details

Printing Options:

❋ **Digital:** This is the most cost-effective method, and it is often used for do-it-yourself invitation printing; it is also known as ink jet or digital printing.

❋ **Engraving:** In this method, the paper is stamped between the printing plate and a hard surface, producing raised type on the front and indentations on the reverse side.

❋ **Letterpress:** In this method, the paper is pressed to create an impression on the paper, giving a luxurious, textured feel.

❋ **Offset printing:** In this commonly used technique, an inked impression is transferred from a plate to a rubber cylinder and then to paper, giving a flat image.

❋ **Thermography:** This method gives the look of engraving, but it uses a powder ink and heat to create a raised surface on the paper without indentations on the back.

Samples of Invitation Wording

■ Bride's parents hosting with the ceremony at a house of worship:

Mr. and Mrs. Brian Edwards

request the honor of your presence at the marriage of their daughter

Joanna Elizabeth to Jude Alexander Smith

Saturday, the eighteenth of May, two thousand and thirteen,
at half past five in the afternoon

Saint Mark's Church, Durham, North Carolina

Reception to follow

■ Bride's parents hosting with the ceremony at a nonreligious venue:

Mr. and Mrs. Brock Stevens

request the pleasure of your company at the marriage of their daughter

Erica Anna to Craig Mason Nelson
Son of Mr. and Mrs. Scott Nelson

Saturday, the fifteenth of June, two thousand and thirteen,
at six in the evening

Middleton Place Plantation, Charleston, South Carolina

Reception to follow

■ Both sets of parents hosting with the ceremony at a house of worship:

Mr. and Mrs. Adam Sanders
and Mr. and Mrs. Mark Peterson

request the honor of your presence at the marriage of their children

Sadie Tyler to Joshua Owen Peterson

Saturday, the fifteenth of June, two thousand and thirteen,
at six in the evening

United Methodist Church, Augusta, Georgia

Reception to follow

■ Both sets of parents hosting with the ceremony at a nonreligious venue:

Mr. and Mrs. Thomas Clark
and Mr. and Mrs. Preston Smith

request the pleasure of your company at the marriage of their children

Kelly Diana to Charles Preston Smith

Saturday, the eighteenth of May, two thousand and thirteen,
at half past five in the afternoon

The Bowery Hotel, New York, New York

Dinner and dancing to follow

■ Bridal couple hosting with the ceremony at a house of worship:

Together with their parents

Allison Kathryn Jones
and Joseph Robert Parker

Request the pleasure of your company at the celebration of their marriage

Saturday, the fifteenth of June, two thousand and thirteen,
at six in the evening

Peach Tree Baptist Church, Atlanta, Georgia

Dinner and dancing to follow

■ Bridal couple hosting with ceremony at a nonreligious venue:

Together with their parents

Brittany Marie Wentworth
and Douglas H. Prescott

Request the pleasure of your company at the celebration of their marriage

Saturday, the eighteenth of May, two thousand and thirteen,
at half past five in the afternoon

Inn at Blackberry Farm, Walland, Tennessee

Dinner and dancing to follow

■ One set of divorced parents hosting jointly with the ceremony at a house of worship:

Mr. and Mrs. Brady Levine

and Ms. Genevieve Cooper

Request the honor of your presence at the marriage of their daughter

Sarah Elizabeth Levine to Gabe Nicholas Sparber

Saturday, the ninth of November, two thousand and thirteen,

at seven in the evening

6th & I Synagogue, Washington, District of Columbia

Reception to follow

Invitation Worksheet

☐ The names of the people hosting the wedding or issuing the invitation: _____

_____

☐ Request for presence: _____

_____

☐ Bride's and groom's full names: _____

_____

☐ Date and time: _____

_____

☐ Ceremony location: _____

_____

☐ Dress code (if applicable): _____

_____

☐ Reply card (if applicable): _____

_____

☐ Reception information: _____

_____

☐ Other information: _____

_____

Working with a Calligrapher and Addressing Invitations

There is nothing more personal than receiving an invitation that has been hand-addressed in beautiful calligraphy. If you want to provide this experience for your guests, you will need to plan ahead and allow plenty of time to find the right calligrapher to fit your needs, style, and budget.

Selecting Your Calligrapher

Before you order your save-the-date announcement and/or wedding invitations, ask the staff of local stationery and bridal stores for recommendations for a calligrapher. You will probably find a variety of talented professionals who provide this service, and they book quickly—so allow plenty of time to talk with several and see samples of their work.

Here are a few things to consider when selecting and working with a calligrapher.

■ Some calligraphers charge "per line," while others charge "per card or envelope." Have a firm understanding of how each potential calligrapher charges, and make sure those costs fit your budget before you select someone.

■ Calligraphers differ in how they want to receive the guest names and mailing information—some prefer to have the information sorted into columns in an Excel document (similar to your guest list tracker), while others prefer the information just as you wish it to appear on the envelope. Ask ahead of time about your calligrapher's preference.

■ Before you order your invitations, confirm the amount of extra envelopes and other supplies your calligrapher would like to have on hand to cover writing mistakes and invitations that might be returned due to address changes. Being prepared will allow speedy corrections.

words of wisdom: Understandably, handwritten professional calligraphy may not be in everyone's budget. If you do not feel that the investment is best for the overall vision of your wedding, consider asking a family member or friend who has nice handwriting to address the envelopes. You might also opt to have the envelopes printed using a computer and home printer, but avoid printing the addresses on an office-style label sheet. You don't want the envelopes to look mass-produced, which can make guests feel like they are receiving a bulk-mail piece.

- If you are planning to use the same calligrapher for your escort cards or other day-of paper goods, confirm the amount of lead time needed to do these items on time. The time requirement may affect your RSVP date.

- As soon as you order your invitation suite, show a sample to your calligrapher and work together to determine the writing style and ink color to complement the font and style on your invitation and other printed pieces. Keep in mind that these variables might affect what the calligrapher charges.

- If you want your calligrapher to write your names, the date, or perhaps all of the text for your invitation suite, you will need to plan ahead. The printing plates that will be made from the handwritten text take time to produce, so be mindful of the date the stationer needs those elements to have the invitation suite printed on time.

Formatting Your Guest Tracker for Your Calligrapher

Creating your calligraphy list will be a breeze if you have a thorough and well-maintained guest list tracker. Regardless of how busy you may become during your engagement, this is one ongoing wedding-planning effort that should be at the top of your priority list (see Chapter 1). When created correctly, your guest list will serve as an easy and accurate reference for almost every vendor involved in your wedding planning, especially your calligrapher.

When it comes to providing each guest's information, remember to do your very best to set up your selected professional for success. Provide as much information as possible and, if necessary, explain in detail what you want written. Be sure to write out every word to avoid abbreviations, double-check the spelling of each guest's name, confirm each address, and be sure to include the zip code. If you are inviting some of your family and friends to bring a guest, do your best to find out the names of the extra guests before you give your list to your calligrapher.

make it yours

Consider having a rubber stamp made with your names or a small wedding-brand related icon. It is a cost-effective way to personalize items used before, during, and after your wedding.

To help provide clear guidance to your calligrapher, consider presenting the information in the following format:

Outside Envelope – married couple
Mr. and Mrs. Curtis Bryan
123 North Columbus Street
Alexandria, Virginia
22314

Escort Card
Mr. and Mrs. Curtis Bryan

Outside Envelope – a dating couple, not living together (send one to each person)
Ms. Kate Williams
1210 White Bridge Road
Bloomfield Hills, Michigan
48302

Escort Card
Ms. Kate Williams
Mr. Paul Raynes

Outside Envelope – single person with a guest of his or her choice
Ms. Brittany Kent and Guest
387 Exeter Street
Unit 207
Boston, Massachusetts
02216

Escort Card
Ms. Brittany Kent
Mr. John Price

Outside Envelope – unmarried couple living together
Ms. Lauren O'Reilly
Mr. Devin Cole
15 Sage Brush Terrace
Apartment 4B
Arlington, Virginia
22201

Escort Card
Ms. Lauren O'Reilly
Mr. Devin Cole

Outside Envelope – family with children under 18
Mr. and Mrs. Thomas Hardindale and Family
15 Mount Pleasant Drive
Concord, New Hampshire
03301

Escort Card
Mr. and Mrs. Thomas Hardindale
Theodore and Samantha

Outside Envelope – couple where woman is a doctor
Mr. and Doctor John Cameron
6 University Boulevard
Durham, New Hampshire
48302

Escort Card
Mr. John Cameron and Doctor Laura Cameron

Outside Envelope – couple where man is a doctor
Dr. and Mrs. Clark Lee
4875 Clark Street, Northwest
Washington, District of Columbia
20002

Escort Card
Dr. and Mrs. Clark Lee

Sample if using your guest list tracker in Excel:

Outside Envelope Addressed to	Inside Envelope Addressed to	Address line one	Address line two	City	State	Zip Code	Notes
Mr. and Mrs. Curtis Hall	Mr. and Mrs. Curtis Hall	123 North Columbus Street	Apartment 4B	Alexandria	Virginia	22314	

Selecting and Preparing Day-of Paper Goods

Welcome Bag: Aside from your save-the-date announcements and/or invitations, the first glance your out-of-town guests may have of your wedding branding is your welcome bag they receive when they check into their hotel rooms. Welcome bags are by no means required, but guests who have traveled to be with you certainly will appreciate them. Include additional information about wedding-related events in your welcome bags, as well as some hospitality-related items to make their stay more comfortable.

Personalize your welcome bags and contents to reflect the location of your wedding and/or perhaps your hometown favorites. Here are a few ideas.

■ **A convenient container:** Before you buy a non-disposable container, remember that your guests will need to take the item home with them.

■ **Welcome note:** Let your guests know how happy and appreciative you are that they came to celebrate your special day with you. If you don't want to take the time to handwrite your welcome notes—consider having your stationer print a general message on the note cards you have chosen and leave space at the bottom for a brief personal note and your signature.

■ **Agenda:** For a quick reference in case a guest forgot to bring your invitation and does not have Internet access to check your wedding Web site for information, be sure to outline what to expect and where

words of wisdom:
If you hope that guests will reuse the welcome bag itself, consider omitting your names and wedding date. No matter how nice the bag, no one really wants to carry a tote that has someone else's name on it.

to be throughout your wedding weekend. Guests will appreciate being informed and having the opportunity to prepare for the various events. If your ceremony is outside by the water, suggest that ladies might want to bring a shawl and other helpful tips. If your guests will have some downtime, include a list of local sightseeing spots and great restaurants. Also let your guests know if transportation will be provided, from what location, and at what time(s).

■ **Snacks and convenience items:** Think about the items you would want to receive when you check into a hotel room. Whether you offer a small sweet treat or a bag full of hometown snacks and souvenirs, your guests will appreciate your thoughtful hospitality.

To help you determine how many welcome bags to prepare and how much to spend on each one, think about the following.

☐ **Quantity:** Do you want to offer one bag per person, one per couple, or one per family?_____

☐ **Value:** Is the real takeaway and gift the bag itself or the contents?_____

☐ **Hotel fees:** Will the hotel charge a handling/delivery fee? This can be up to a few dollars per bag._____

☐ **Extra packaging:** Will you be buying the items for the bags in bulk and placing the items in smaller containers?_____

☐ **Personalization:** Will you be adding personalized tags or wrappers? Who will prepare these items?_____

☐ **Delivery:** Are you planning to deliver the bags to the hotel(s), or will you need to recruit a family member or friend or hire someone else to do it?_____

make it yours
Get creative!

Personalize ordinary bottles of water by removing the label and adding a strip of paper that complements the rest of your branded wedding paper goods. If you are including homemade or other special items, let guests know their significance by adding a descriptive tag, such as Grandma Sally's Homemade Cookies, tied with ribbon in one of your wedding colors. Your efforts will not go unnoticed!

Wedding Ceremony Program: The program not only serves as a guide for guests during your ceremony, but it also offers the perfect opportunity to highlight your family, bridal party, and special ceremonial wedding traditions. Styling of wedding ceremony programs varies widely—some are small booklets that outline everything from people to traditions, while others are simple cards that just list the order of the ceremony. If your ceremony is in a house of worship, contact your officiant first to discuss what should be included in your program, and keep in mind that some religious institutions ask to approve the ceremony program before it goes to the printer. Also remember that for many guests, the program will be another keepsake from your wedding. Take your time writing the text and make it as simple or in depth as you like.

Here are some elements that you may want to include:

- [ ] The location of the ceremony, the date, and the time
- [ ] A dedication or "in honor or remembrance of" message
- [ ] The names of your parents and grandparents
- [ ] The names of (and perhaps your relationship to) each member of your bridal party
- [ ] The names of the officiant(s), greeters, ushers, readers, soloists, musicians, and any other participants
- [ ] The outline of the wedding ceremony
- [ ] The readings, hymns, and other participatory components
- [ ] A description of specific religious or cultural traditions that will be included
- [ ] A thank-you from the two of you
- [ ] Your new home address

words of wisdom: If you are not working with a wedding planner, alphabetize your escort cards before you give them to your caterer or venue representative. Also give your caterer or venue representative two copies of your guest list, one with the names in alphabetical order and the other by table number or table name—this will make it easy for them to help guests who lose their escort cards or need assistance finding their tables.

Escort Cards, Seating Charts, and Place Cards: Escort cards, personalized cards sometimes placed inside business card-size envelopes, direct guests to their table assignments. Traditionally the name of the guest is handwritten on the accompanying envelope—you may want to have your calligrapher do this for you. You may also want to incorporate the escort cards, arranged alphabetically, into a pleasing display in keeping with your wedding colors and style.

Not all couples use escort cards. Instead, you may want to have the names of all of your guests and their table assignments written on a large seating chart decorated in your wedding colors and style.

Table Numbers and Table Names: Most caterers or banquet facilities provide plastic table numbers. Although these are convenient, consider using table numbers or perhaps table names that have a more personalized look instead. Cards that complement your invitation suite with handwritten numbers or names will soften the look of your tables and add another layer of personalized detail. Remember that the table number or table name should be written on both sides of each card—this will be especially helpful if guests will be entering the room through more than one entry.

■ Ideas for table numbers or table names:

☐ Meaningful dates from your relationship (for example, June 28—Paul proposed)

☐ Places you have lived as a couple

☐ Your favorite places to travel

■ Ideas for displaying table numbers or table names:

☐ The numbers spelled out and handwritten, perhaps by your calligrapher, on a tent card

☐ Individual metal or wooden house numbers leaning against the centerpiece

☐ The numbers or names handwritten or printed on a paper or felt pennant

☐ The numbers or names on decals adhered to the container of the floral centerpiece

You can be as creative or classic as you like—just make sure your ideas tie back to your Buzz Words (page 14), Inspiration Board (page 32), and your wedding colors and style.

If you are not offering a full bar, consider creating a drink menu, either a small printed sign or a large handwritten board, to let guests know what special beverages are being offered. Creating a drink menu will make your selections look more like a careful decision rather than a cost-saving measure.

Menu Cards: Regardless of what type of wedding meal you choose to offer, it is practical to give your guests some information about the delicious meal they are about to enjoy. Offering a printed menu will let guests know what to expect so they can make their waiter aware in advance of any potential allergies or diet needs.

Traditionally menu cards are placed on or tucked into the napkin at each place setting. You may choose to offer one or two menu cards per table or, in the case of a buffet-style meal, showcase a large menu board of the items available on the buffet. Don't overlook the opportunity to personalize your menu card or board! Your guests will enjoy knowing about local ingredients used in the dishes, specialty preparations, and any family favorite recipes that are being served.

Miscellaneous Printed Details

You may want to consider including other classic printed components, such as cocktail napkins, coasters, matchbooks, smaller favors, and directional signage, into your personalized wedding paper products. You can choose from a variety of online resources for these items, and many companies offer a range of pre-designed options for you to select from and customize.

Here are a few ideas for you to consider featuring on small printed items for your reception.

- ◼ Fun trivia about the two of you _____
  _____
  _____

- ◼ A logo that combines a graphic with your initials _____
  _____
  _____

- ◼ A classic monogram of your names _____
  _____
  _____

- ◼ A signature drink recipe _____
  _____
  _____
  _____
  _____
  _____
  _____
  _____

Toward the end of your reception time, place a small sign at the coat-check room or bar that lists the transportation schedule or the names and numbers of local taxicab companies to help ensure that no one is left stranded!

Items	Order Quantity	Lead Time to Produce
Save-the-Date	Dictated by guest list + 10% overage 20% extra on envelopes	Mail at least 6 months before if destination; can take up to 8 weeks to produce
Invitations	Dictated by guest list + 10% overage 20% extra on envelopes	Ordering based on supplier—the sooner the better Allow 2 weeks for calligraphy Mail 8 weeks before the wedding RSVPs due 4 weeks before
Ceremony Programs	Decide if you will offer 1 per guest or 1 per couple and order accordingly	May be prepared as early as possible but ordered by or just after RSVP date
Escort Cards	1 per couple plus 1 per single guest, + 20% extra	Allow at least 2 weeks for calligraphy
Place Cards	1 per person + 20% extra	Send to calligrapher with escort cards
Menu Cards	1 per person + 20% extra	1 month before

Items	Quantity Ordered	Date Ordered
Save-the-Date		
Invitations		
Ceremony Programs		
Escort Cards		
Place Cards		
Menu Cards		

Thank-you Stationery

It is beyond important to make sure that you prepare (and have readily available) proper thank-you stationery. You may personalize these note cards to complement your invitation suite, or you may want to purchase notes that are a bit more timeless (omitting your wedding date from these cards will allow you to use them for occasions well beyond your special day). You may want to consider having two separate sets of cards produced for your pre-wedding and post-wedding needs, especially if you will be changing your name or moving to a different address. Regardless of what type of thank-you notes you choose, remember that, generally speaking, it is polite to send a written expression of your gratitude within two weeks of receiving a gift or attending an event. A gracious hostess or host will let no act of kindness, big or small, go unnoticed.

Southern touch

There's nothing quite so refreshing as a Southern signature drink. Typical favorites include Mint Julep, Bloody Mary, and Mojitos, just to name a few. Also consider creating your own signature drink using a favorite Southern ingredient such as lemonade, sweet tea, or bourbon.

Whether you have chosen an elaborate custom letter-press invitation or a modest design available online, all of the paper goods you choose for your wedding should be an expression of your special day—and they should leave your guests with the impression that "This is so them!"

Emily Monroe
TABLE N° 2

3

Menu

JENNIFER & ALEX

STARTER

Buffalo Caprese
FRESH MOZZARELLA
WITH GRAPE TOMATOES
AND BASIL

Arugula Salad
BABY ARUGULA WITH
GRAPE TOMATOES
AND PARMIGIANO

MAIN

Salmone Alla Griglia
GRILLED ORGANIC SCOTTISH SALMON
SERVED WITH SAUTÉED ESCAROLE
AND CANNELLONI BEANS

Pollo al Mattone
ROASTED ORGANIC AMISH CHICKEN
SERVED WITH ROASTED POTATOES, CIPOLLINI
ONIONS AND FRISÉE GREENS

Tagliata
GRILLED GRASS-FED RIBEYE STEAK,
SLICED AND SERVED OVER ROASTED POTATOES,
CIPOLLINI ONIONS AND FRISÉE GREENS

Desserts

Chocolate Tartlets GARNISHED WITH RASPBERRY
Lemon Bars
Chewy Chocolate Chip Cookie Sandwiches
WITH CREAM CHEESE
Chocolate Dipped Profiteroles
FILLED WITH PASTRY CREAM

KINDLY RESPOND
by the 20th of March

M

ACCEPTS WITH PLEASURE
DECLINES WITH REGRETS

Flowers

The floral arrangements you choose for your wedding will set the scene and help bring your vision to life. The flowers not only will showcase the style and colors you prefer, but their natural beauty and fragrance also will enhance the romantic ambience.

Once you settle on the overall look and color palette, start paying attention to the flowers you see during your everyday activities, at special occasions, and in magazines. Keep a list of the specific flowers, including colors, as well as floral arrangements you like. Find out the names of the floral designers. Also notice the shape and size of various arrangements, the containers used, and the specific flowers, greenery, and color and bloom combinations.

When you have an idea of what you prefer, research the florists you admire. Make appointments with a few whose styles complement the look you want. Although most floral designers are extremely talented and able to achieve a variety of looks, most have a niche in terms of style.

Working with a Florist

Your first meeting with a florist entails discussing the overall look of your wedding and specific ideas you have so far. Be sure to bring your planning binder, the lists of flowers and arrangements you like, and any photos you have gathered. Also bring photos or illustrations of your dress, the attire your groom and the members of your bridal party will wear, and your ceremony and reception venues, if possible. In addition, decide ahead of time the approximate total amount you want to spend on flowers, keeping in mind that you will be paying for the blooms as well as the time and talent of your floral designer.

Each florist you meet with should show you his or her portfolio and give you detailed information about the different flowers mentioned so you can make appropriate choices from the somewhat intimidating list of available flower options. Be sure to ask each florist to show you various styles and sizes of centerpieces and other arrangements so you have a clear understanding of the difference between a $100 and a $500 floral piece. If you are on a tight budget, ask each florist for advice on what your priorities should be based on your wish list and what options you might consider.

Questions to ask a florist

Questions	Florist Name: _____	Florist Name: _____	Florist Name: _____
Are you available on our date?			
How many weddings do you generally book per weekend?			
Can you provide candelabras, candles, unique containers, and other accessories, such as an aisle runner and chuppah?			
Have you done a wedding at our venue(s)?			
What are the steps in working together?			

Most florists provide information about floral arrangements in the following three categories, and they will include descriptive elements for each item. (For more information, see "Selecting Your Bridal Bouquet" on page 178.)

- **Personal Flowers:** bride's bouquet(s); bridesmaids' bouquets; groom's boutonniere(s); groomsmen's boutonnieres; parents', grandparents', and godparents' flowers (such as corsages and nosegays); children's flowers (such as hair wreaths, pomanders, and flower baskets); and pieces for ushers, readers, and any other special participants you want to honor

- **Ceremony Flowers:** altar plinths and arrangements; aisle markers and arrangements; chuppah decorations; arrangements for entrances, doors, and any other areas that may need to be decorated (such as steps or a walkway)

- **Reception Flowers:** cocktail hour, escort card display, dinner table centerpieces, favor tables, food/dessert stations, and bar

Along with the cost of the floral pieces, be sure you understand what labor and delivery/pick up fees and taxes will be included in the total amount. Also, ask if the containers used for the floral arrangements are included in the total and can be kept, or if they are considered rental items and must be returned.

Cost-Cutting Considerations

■ **Select flowers that are in season.** Even though peonies are gorgeous, they are not always in season; if they are out of season in your area, they will probably need to be flown in from another location, making them more expensive. Ask your florist about available seasonal options or alternative flowers before you set your heart on a flower that might break your budget. (Please see "Flowers and Seasonal Availability" on page 176.)

■ **"Simple" does not mean inexpensive.** Remember that a simple floral arrangement does not necessarily mean it will cost less than a more elaborate or structured piece.

■ **Use floral pieces more than once.** Try to use a floral arrangement several times, such as moving the cocktail hour arrangements to the food/dessert tables for the reception. Also ask your florist about the option of using one or more of the ceremony or reception arrangements (or modified versions of them) for the brunch(es) or other events.

■ **Use one large "impact" piece.** Consider investing in one floral statement arrangement, such as a large, eye-catching piece for the escort card table or a bar, instead of including floral arrangements on each dinner table.

■ **Consider using nonblooming pieces.** Potted herbs, topiaries, garlands, and fruit can give a beautiful look without breaking your budget.

■ **Pick your own blooms.** Many areas have pick-your-own wildflower farms that are open in the summer and early fall, as well as flower markets where you can purchase fresh flowers. If you want to create your own bouquet(s), be sure to use only a few types of well-conditioned flowers—and also be sure to take on this project only if you truly have time to do it. You will already be plenty busy with other preparations!

■ **Be mindful of holidays.** If your wedding date is close to Valentine's, Mother's Day, Christmas, or other holidays, flowers may be more expensive, depending on demand.

	Florist Name:	Florist Name:	Florist Name:
Estimate			
Price includes			

Following your initial meeting, each florist should send you a proposal that includes specific pricing or price ranges based on the types of flowers and pieces you discussed. If you are considering more than one florist, be sure to carefully compare not only prices but also the descriptions of each piece. If you are having a tough time choosing one of the florists, go back to your Four Ss and Buzz Words (pages 13 and 14) to help you decide which one can best create floral pieces in the style you want.

Once you book your florist, you probably will be able to fine-tune the details of the floral arrangements up to a month before your wedding. Most florists need the final table count and any last-minute changes before they place the floral order three to four weeks before the date.

Flowers and Seasonal Availability

Flower	Colors	Season
Amaryllis	white/cream, red, pink	winter
Anemone	white/cream, purple, blue, red, pink	early winter, spring, early summer
Billy Button	yellow	all seasons
Carnation	white/cream, deep purple, pink, red, orange, yellow, green	all seasons
Cherry Blossom	white/cream, pink	spring
Chrysanthemum	white/cream, purple, pink, red, orange, yellow, green	all seasons
Daffodil	white/cream, orange, yellow	spring
Dahlia	white/cream, purple, pink, red, orange, yellow	late summer, fall
Daisy	white/cream	all seasons
Delphinium	white/cream, blue, purple	spring, summer
Dusty Miller	green, silver	all seasons
Eucalyptus	green	all seasons
Freesia	white/cream, purple, pink, yellow	all seasons
Fiddlehead	green, brown	early spring
Gardenia	white/cream	winter, early summer
Hyacinth	white/cream, blue, purple, pink, yellow	spring
Hydrangea	white/cream, blue, purple, pink, green	all seasons
Iris	white/cream, blue, purple	all seasons
Lamb's Ear	green, silver	all seasons

Flower	Colors	Season
Lavender	purple	spring, summer, fall
Lilac	white/cream, purple	spring
Lily	white/cream	all seasons
Lily of the Valley	white/cream	spring
Lissanthus	white/cream, purple, pink, green	all seasons
Magnolia	white/cream	late spring, summer
Orchid (Cymbidium)	white/cream, purple, pink, yellow, green, orange	all seasons
Peony	white/cream, pink	spring
Poppy	pink, red, orange, yellow	spring
Ranunculus	white/cream, pink, red, orange, yellow, green	winter, spring
Rose (Cabbage)	white/cream, pink	fall, winter, spring
Rose (David Austin)	white/cream, purple, pink, red, orange, yellow, green	all seasons
Rose (Juliet)	white/cream, pink, red, orange	all seasons
Snapdragon	white/cream	all seasons
Stephanotis	white/cream	winter
Stock	white/cream, purple, green	spring, summer, fall
Sunflower	yellow, orange	summer, fall
Sweet Pea	white/cream, pink	late winter, spring
Thistle	purple, green	summer, fall
Tulip (French)	white/cream, purple, pink, red, orange, yellow, green,	spring, winter
Tulip (Parrot)	white/cream, purple, pink, red orange, yellow, green,	spring, winter
Viburnum	white/cream	spring

Southern touch

Unique Seasonal Floral Options

Spring: branches of apple, cherry, dogwood, forsythia, orange, and quince blossoms

Summer: peegee and oakleaf hydrangeas, lemons, limes, and succulents

Fall: cotton bolls, berry branches, curly willow, fig branches, gourds, and pumpkins

Winter: berry branches, cranberries, evergreen garland, pinecones, pomegranates, and snowberries

Selecting Your Bridal Bouquet

For most brides, their wedding day is the first time they will carry a gorgeous bouquet designed just for them. You will cherish your bouquet even more if it complements your dress and accessories and completes your wedding day vision. Be sure to show your florist photos of your dress and fabric swatches, if you have them, so he or she will have a good understanding of the look you prefer and be able to design your bouquet so it enhances your personal style.

words of wisdom: The all-white bouquet is lovely, but be sure your florist allows for enough texture as well as slight variations in color to keep your bouquet from blending into your dress in photographs.

Shapes of Bridal Bouquets

Cascading	Hand-Tied	Heart	Nosegay	Pomander
This large-scale bouquet is composed of flowers that have been wired together to create extended length.	Many brides are now requesting this type of bouquet, which derives its name from the way the floral designer composes it.	The flowers in this type of bouquet are arranged in a heart shape, with the point of the heart facing downward.	This popular style has a globe-like shape and contains a limited variety of blooms that are either concentrated and tight or loose and airy.	This style features a tight "ball" of flowers that hangs from a loop of ribbon, making it a perfect option for a flower girl.

Posy	Round	Shield	Toss	Tussie-Mussie
This bouquet is a well-edited collection of just a few blooms, which makes it perfect for mothers to carry.	In this style, the flowers are arranged to create a visually round shape, like a ball.	This style, which Catherine Middleton made popular when she carried it for her recent marriage to Prince William, is a dainty shield-shaped arrangement that accentuates the bride's waistline.	This small-scale version of the bride's bouquet, perhaps featuring only one type of flower, is the bouquet the bride will toss away at the end of the reception.	This small-scale grouping of flowers is similar to a posy, but it is contained in a metal cone that hides the stems.

Personalizing Your Bridal Bouquet

Some brides like to make a personal statement that goes beyond pretty flowers by adding a sentimental charm or memento to their bouquets. From a monogrammed handkerchief to a vintage locket, here are a few ways to personalize your special bouquet.

Heirlooms: Your bouquet offers the perfect place to incorporate "something borrowed." You may want to hold your bouquet with a special handkerchief or wrap the stems with a piece of fabric from your mother's wedding gown. Pinning a family brooch to the stem of your bouquet will add sentiment as well as a touch of glamour.

Monograms: You may choose to follow the age-old Southern tradition of adding a handkerchief or ribbon with your new initials and/or wedding date.

Lockets: Honor the memory of a special family member by displaying their photo in a locket casually but securely pinned to the stems of the flowers in your bouquet.

Sentimental Touches: You may want to add sentimental meaning to your special day by carrying blooms from your mother's garden or the same flowers that your mother or grandmother carried.

Tying Styles: You can choose to have the stems of your bouquet show or concealed. Consider having a ribbon tied corset style around the stems to add texture and interest, or have them completely wrapped in satin for a smooth, formal finish.

Flowers for Your Bridesmaids and Mothers

A nice way for you to honor the important ladies in your life is by giving them special flowers to wear or carry on your wedding day.

Bridesmaids often carry a bouquet similar in style to the bride's but of a smaller scale and simpler design. The bouquets should complement the bridesmaids' dresses and your wedding Buzz Words (page 14). You will have unlimited design options to choose from for these handheld arrangements and plenty of ways to personalize the blooms for each attendant. Consider adding their initials or monograms to the bouquet wrap or having each attendant carry a single flower that is used in your bouquet.

When it comes to the mothers of the bride and groom, more and more brides are choosing small posies of meaningful blooms for them to carry. You might consider having your mother carry the same blooms that she carried on her wedding day! A more traditional option is to give mothers a wrist or pin-on corsage.

Flowers for Your Groom and Groomsmen

When planning for your floral needs, don't forget about the gentlemen! The boutonniere is a small work of art that usually echoes the flowers in the bride's or bridesmaids' bouquets or centerpieces. When selecting a bloom for your groom and his attendants, be sure to keep the colors of his tie and suit or tuxedo in mind. Just like your bridal bouquet, your groom's flower should accent his overall styling rather than be eye-catching. For consistency, select one floral style for all of your groom's attendants, your and his fathers, grandfathers, godfathers, and ushers. Choose a slightly more designed look for your groom. You can choose to have the stems wrapped in a handsome ribbon, or you can tuck them neatly into his lapel buttonhole. Remember to keep scale in mind when making your selection—you don't want an oversize boutonniere to spoil the overall look and style of the attire.

details, details, details

Consider ordering two boutonnieres for your groom so if something happens to the original, you have a backup. With all the hugging, having a spare will ensure that it will look picture perfect.

How To Pin On a Boutonniere

1. Place the boutonniere on the left side of the lapel with the flower on or just below the broadest part.

2. From the back of the lapel, position the pin so the head is under the lapel, and push the point up through the fabric, "catch" the stem of the boutonniere, and then push it down under the lapel.

3. Once you are sure that the boutonniere is secure and the pin is not showing, you are ready for the ceremony and photos.

Flowers for Your Ceremony

The most beautiful part of your wedding will undoubtedly be the ceremony. Whether you choose to add or omit floral decorations from this part of the day depends on your style, preferences, and budget. Many houses of worship are structurally beautiful enough and may not need or allow live floral decorations. Some outside locations already provide a desirable backdrop, but they might require some floral decorations beyond your personal flowers to help define the space and add a focal point. No matter how you choose to decorate your ceremony venue or what floral elements you decide to include, remember that these creative components should enhance, rather than distract from, the setting, mood, and style you want for your special day.

Here are a few things to consider when you are deciding how to enhance your ceremony venue with floral pieces:

Your Vision

☐ *What does your dream ceremony location look like defined by your Buzz Words and Inspiration Board?*

☐ *Do you want the flowers and floral arrangements to accent your ceremony or be focal points?*

☐ *If your ceremony will be outside, do your floral decorations need to be designed with a "rain plan space" in mind?*

☐ *What is your budget?*

Playing by the Rules

☐ *If you are to be married in a house of worship, are live flowers from an outside vendor allowed, or are you required to use the venue's sources? Are you required to leave any of the floral arrangements as a donation?*

☐ *What traditional or religious elements, such as a chuppah, do you want to incorporate? Do they need floral decorations?*

☐ *Does the venue or house of worship permit decorations to be hung on doors or the sides of pews or chairs?*

☐ *Are you allowed to use aisle decorations, such as an aisle runner?*

Creating Your Decorating Plan

First decide what floral elements you want to include. Be sure to share your ideas when you meet with the florists you are considering, and also ask for their advice (please see "Working with a Florist" on page 172). Here are some options to consider.

Entrance Wreaths: You may want to decorate the doors or entrance to your ceremony venue with either traditional floral/greenery wreaths or "wreaths" of greenery in the shape of your and your groom's initials. This welcoming design element will add a thoughtful touch of classic style and also help set the scene.

Aisle Runner: The original purpose of the aisle runner dates back to the days of unfinished floors, when it protected the bride's gown from getting dirty; the runner was rolled down the aisle just before the bride processed. Today's aisle runners come in a wide variety of customized fabrics and span the length of the aisle. Politely reserved for the entrance of members of the processional and the bride, this decorative treatment both adds interest and creates a visual path. Surprisingly, many venues and houses of worship now have rules prohibiting aisle runners because the fabric, which is not attached to the floor or carpeting under it, poses a potential tripping hazard. If your ceremony venue allows an aisle runner, ask your florist if he or she can provide one for you, what fabric options are available, and the cost. If your venue does not allow a fabric runner or if you decide you don't want one, consider highlighting the sides of the aisle with pretty petals or tall glass cylinders filled with pillar candles—both options will provide a lovely accent and may be incorporated into the design of the floral pew or chair markers.

■ **Pew or Chair Markers:** These small floral arrangements hang from the sides of pews or chairs to add decoration to the center aisle. Some brides choose to limit the number of floral markers to just the "reserved" seats, which adds a visual notation that these are for special guests. Find out if your ceremony venue allows floral markers or has any restrictions on using them. If they are allowed, ask your florist to help you select or design appropriate pieces within your budget.

■ **Altar Floral Arrangements:** Floral arrangements for the altar, which are used to define where the bride, groom, and officiant will stand, are usually placed on either side of the area around the altar. They are large in scale and sit on plinths, such as columns, pedestals, or structure bases. The plinths elevate the arrangements, adding height and making the scale of the pieces feel more in line with the scale of the venue.

■ **Chuppah:** A chuppah, the canopy under which a Jewish couple traditionally stands during their wedding ceremony, symbolizes the home the couple will build together. It consists of a cloth, called a tallis, that is supported by four poles. The styling of chuppahs varies, but they are usually draped with lush flowers. Many non-Jewish couples have begun to incorporate this meaningful tradition into their ceremonies, and they put quite a bit of effort into making the chuppah a focal point of the ceremony venue. If you want to include a chuppah, consider the location where it will stand, and work with your florist on the style and floral decoration. If you are planning to have your ceremony outdoors, be sure that the structure is stable and grounded. Also have a rain plan and some easy adaptations that can be made in case you need to move the ceremony inside.

words of wisdom: If you have to return the flower containers to your florist, provide waxed tissue paper and twine or ribbon so your guests can take home some of the lovely flowers after your reception.

Flowers for Your Reception

Your reception venue should serve as inspiration for you and your florist when you select the areas to decorate and the floral pieces that will enhance the spaces. If your florist has not done a wedding reception or another event at the location, arrange for him or her to visit the venue with you to get a firsthand look at architectural elements, such as windows, fireplace mantels, and unique spots that can be highlighted with floral pieces.

Entrances: If your reception will be in a private space, such as a museum, mansion, or home, decorate the door with a pretty wreath or flank the entrance with beautiful plinths topped with eye-catching floral arrangements. If your reception is under an outdoor tent with multiple access points, frame an area that will serve as the main entrance. A pretty garland of magnolia or other blooms draped across the main entrance makes a beautiful and welcoming touch.

Escort Card Display: All of your guests will visit the escort card table to find their seating assignment, and they are sure to notice the floral decoration. An impact floral piece serves as a good investment for this table, and you might want to consider a tall, dramatic arrangement, perhaps one that features branches of cherry, dogwood, or other seasonal blossoms.

Cocktail Hour: You want to leave plenty of space on cocktail tables, which are generally only 2 to 3 feet in diameter, for guests to set down their glasses, plates, cameras, and purses. So consider using small arrangements, such as bud vases with single blooms.

■ **Dinner Table Centerpieces:** Selecting or designing appropriate, within-budget floral arrangements for the dinner tables will probably be one of your most challenging decisions. The cost of the large number of flowers used in these centerpieces will add up quickly, but your guests will spend the longest amount of time during your reception at the dinner tables, so you want the floral decorations to beautifully embody your style and look. Here are some options to consider.

Height	Lush or Airy
 If you like the look of tall arrangements, use them—but be sure your guests will be able to see each other across the table. Consider using narrow floral containers for tall pieces.	 If the flowers are the most important part of your reception decor, you may want to choose lush, full arrangements. If the flowers are just one part of the decor, consider using arrangements with the flowers spread apart for a more airy look.
Collections	Monochromatic
 Talk with your florist about creating interesting vignettes on the dinner tables with multiple containers of different shapes and sizes filled with flowers grouped by types. You can vary the collections at each table to provide an easy, beautiful look that is not too "matchy-matchy."	 For a luxurious look, consider grouping flowers by type and using only one color, such as white or cream.

■ **Other Tables:** Although not all of the tables need a floral decoration, be sure to include bars, food and dessert displays, the cake table, the guest book table, and any other large pieces of furniture.

■ **Fireplaces:** Consider dressing a beautiful fireplace mantel with a mix of floral elements and candles to add a charming touch of warm hospitality.

■ **Your Wedding Cake(s):** If you have selected a cake design that requires or would be enhanced by fresh flowers, be sure to let your florist know so the extra blooms will be ordered with the rest of your flowers. Also be sure to clarify with the bakery if it will be placing the flowers on the cake or if the florist will do it.

Flower Checklist

Wedding Party	Colors	Style	Other Elements	Types of Flowers
Bride				
Maid of honor				
Flower girl				
Bridesmaids				
Junior bridesmaids				
Groom				
Best man				
Groomsmen				
Ring bearer				
Mother of the bride				
Mother of the groom				
Father of the bride				
Father of the groom				
Ushers				
Special friends				

Ceremony	Colors	Style	Other Elements	Types of Flowers
Outside the Ceremony				
Entrance to Ceremony				
Guest Book Table				
Aisle Runner				
Pews				
Steps to Altar or Chuppah				
Altar or Chuppah				
Candles				
Other				

Reception	Colors	Style	Other Elements	Types of Flowers
Outside Reception				
Entrance to Reception				
Head Table				
Guest Tables				
Chairs				
Guest Book Table				
Bar Decorations				
Serving Table Decorations				
Wedding Cake and Table Decorations				
Groom's Cake Table Decorations				
Other				

Your Wedding and Groom's Cakes

The sweetest detail you will work on when you plan your reception is selecting your wedding cake design, flavors, and baker. In fact, your groom will probably look forward to the cake tasting more than other wedding planning meetings!

Start thinking about your wedding cake and groom's cake early in your reception planning process—but wait until after you have settled on an overall look, style, and colors and booked your reception venue before you choose your final cake design and baker. Before you make an appointment with any baker, pay attention to cakes you see at weddings and other events, and find out who made the ones you like. Also look at the photos in this book, as well as in magazines and other resources, to get a clear idea of how you want your cake to look. Plan to meet with two or three bakers who create cakes that you like and get rave reviews for not only beautiful— but also delicious—creations.

make it yours

Be sure to add personal details to your wedding and groom's cakes, as well as to the foods and beverages you choose to offer and the way they are presented and served. Use special local ingredients and feature family recipes and/or dishes the two of you especially enjoy. Include descriptions of the items on the menu card and the story behind each of your selections.

Choosing a Wedding Cake Design and Baker

For your first meeting with a potential baker, be sure to bring your Inspiration Board, photos of cake designs and details that have caught your eye, a photo of your dress, and a motif you might be using on the paper goods that could also be a pretty accent on your cake. If you plan to use a wedding cake topper, such as the one from your parents' or grandparents' wedding cakes, also bring it along—or share those details at your meeting. Much like talking with your florist, you need to use your Buzz Words (page 14) to describe your vision for your special day to potential bakers.

Each baker should show you photos of wedding cakes he or she has created and talk you through available options for the cake shape and tier sizes, as well as how certain flavor and filling selections could influence the design. The baker will also show you available options for decorating the cake, including the types of available icings and decorations like piping patterns, sugar flowers, fondant applications, and other techniques.

In addition, each baker should show you options for displaying your wedding cake. Ask to see the available cake pedestals, or show the baker a photo and size information if you plan to provide the pedestal or other display piece.

Your first meeting should include a tasting where you can sample a variety of cakes, fillings, and icings. At this first tasting, you will probably be offered preselected samplings, but a specialty wedding cake baker should be able to provide incredible options for you to taste later, before you make your final selection—and those selections will surely make your sweet tooth happy.

At the end of your first meeting, ask each baker to give you a proposal that includes a sketch—or a detailed description—of the cake he or she would design for you with your flavor selections per tier.

Questions	Baker Name:	Baker Name:	Baker Name:
What is the name and number of the baker?			
Does the baker provide a tasting?			
What is the price per slice?			
What is the delivery fee?			
Do they require a deposit?			
Do they have alternates to a wedding cake?			
What is the cancellation policy?			

Wedding Cake Worksheet

Budget:_____

Flavor: _____

Fillings: _____

Type of Icing: _____

Decorations: _____

Type of Cake Stand: _____

Cake Serving Set: _____

Groom's Cake Flavor: _____

Groom's Cake Fillings: _____

Groom's Cake Icing: _____

Groom's Cake Decorations: _____

Selecting and Booking Your Baker

Cake bakers structure their pricing per person (or slice). If you are not serving other desserts, plan to purchase a cake large enough to serve all of the people who will be at your reception. If you are serving other desserts, consider ordering a cake large enough to serve 80 percent of the people so you do not pay for leftover cake.

Each baker's proposal will include a delivery fee plus taxes and a penalty fee if you do not return all the pieces of the cake-support system, such as the cake stand or cake board. Some bakers offer a credit, if you book with them, for any fee you paid for the first sample tasting. Bakers typically require a 50 percent deposit to reserve your wedding date, with the remaining 50 percent due on or before the date.

Carefully consider and compare the proposals you receive and ask additional questions, if necessary. Then select a baker who will be able to create a wedding cake that meets your wishes and expectations—and is within your budget.

details, details, details

Work with your cake baker, your reception venue representative, and your caterer to coordinate when your wedding and groom's cakes will be delivered and where they will be stored or placed prior to the time they are cut. Although it is often nice to have your wedding and groom's cakes on display, you may want to avoid this if you are having an outdoor wedding where the sun or heat can cause the cake to sweat or even melt.

Today many couples decide against having a wedding cake and serve an alternative dessert or create fun, personalized dessert displays of mini treats, cupcakes, candy, or even pies.

The Cake-cutting Ceremony

The traditional cake-cutting ceremony symbolizes the first "official task" that you and your husband will complete together. You will share the first piece, perhaps having a little fun doing it.

After the cake-cutting ceremony, the catering staff will probably move the cake out of sight to cut and plate it. Either members of the waitstaff will serve the cake with coffee to the guests, or guests will help themselves at stations.

Be sure to let your caterer know if you will be providing your own special knife and cake-server set, or if you would like them to provide the set for you.

Southern touch

Your Groom's Cake

The groom's cake started as an English wedding tradition and now has become a Southern tradition. The groom's cake, which traditionally is made of chocolate, is presented by the bride as a gift to her groom after the wedding cake is cut. Often the cake design is a surprise, and it can be a playful representation of the groom's favorite sports team or hobby. After the bride cuts the first piece and the couple shares it, members of the catering staff usually cut and serve the groom's cake along with the wedding cake.

words of wisdom: Traditionally the top tier (the smallest) of the cake was set aside at a wedding reception for the bride and groom to take home, store in the freezer, and eat on their first anniversary. Since your cake will taste best on your wedding day, consider skipping an anniversary tier that might get freezer burn—your baker will be glad for you to order a small version of your wedding cake in time for you to enjoy it fresh on your first anniversary.

Your Wedding Reception

Careful thought and planning will help make your wedding reception a beautiful, enjoyable, memorable experience for the two of you, as well as for your family and friends. Just like planning your ceremony and all the other elements of your special day, start with your personal vision for the party where you and your husband will welcome your guests and celebrate the beginning of your married life.

Be sure to keep your Buzz Words (page 14) and Inspiration Board (page 32) in mind when you think about where to have your reception, the time of day (which will depend partly on the time of your ceremony), the food and beverages, the seating arrangements, and all the other details. Make choices that complement the overall look and style you prefer, and add personal touches to make the reception uniquely "yours."

Deciding What Type of Reception You Prefer

Wedding receptions vary widely from late-morning brunches and picnics in the park to cocktail hours followed by elaborate, multicourse, sit-down dinners. If you are on a tight budget, ask your caterer for advice about the type of reception that will give you the best value. Also ask your caterer for food and serving suggestions to help keep costs down.

Depending on the food items you select and the number of people required to prepare and serve them, all of the reception types described below may cost about the same. Food stations usually require more food than the standard serving size per guest to keep the displays looking full and styled. Buffet dinners also usually require extra food to accommodate guests who might help themselves to more of an item than the standard serving size. Although hors d'oeuvres passed by waitstaff and dinners plated by the kitchen staff or composed by waitstaff usually require less food than stations or buffets, these options usually require more people to serve the items.

Here are some details to help you decide which type of reception fits your personal vision—as well as your budget.

Brunch Reception

For many couples, a mid-morning ceremony followed by a stylish late-morning or early-afternoon brunch reception offers a great option. In general, brunch receptions cost less than receptions held later in the day because the foods served are less expensive and the total bar bill is usually less.

Cocktail Reception

Consider a cocktail reception if you are planning a late-afternoon or evening ceremony. Cocktail receptions usually cost less than buffet or seated dinner receptions, unless you plan elaborate food and beverage displays and stations. Consider offering hors d'oeuvres passed by servers—this not only will help reduce the total cost, but it will also work well for any number of guests. A cocktail reception ideally lasts two to three hours, but if you are planning to have a dinner party afterward, limit it to one hour. The rule of thumb is for a cocktail reception to last long enough for guests to have a beverage, enjoy a few passed hors d'oeuvres, and casually mingle—if the reception lasts longer, guests may start to get hungry and restless.

Dinner Reception

You have several serving styles to consider for a dinner reception, and each option can be as simple or elaborate as your wants, needs, and budget dictate. A dinner reception usually follows an hour-long cocktail reception and lasts three to five hours.

☐ Buffet Style

Buffets provide a nice way to please different palettes because guests can choose from a variety of food selections presented all together. In addition, buffet receptions can be a bit more budget friendly if the foods you choose require minimal staff to prepare and display.

☐ Family Style

This style dinner creates a conversational, family ambience as the guests at each dinner table pass platters of food to one another. Family-style receptions can cost more than buffet receptions because they require additional serving platters and utensils. In addition, a larger amount of food may be required because the guests serve themselves and may take more than a standard serving size.

☐ French Service Style

At this style dinner, members of the waitstaff compose the entrée plate for each guest, one at a time, from a large platter or tableside cart that holds a beautiful display of all of the dish's components. French service requires more waitstaff than family-style dinners.

Menu

from the bay, farm & garden

BROILED MARYLAND CRAB CAKES

FRESH-SHUCKED KENT ISLAND OYSTERS

COUNTRY HAM & SWEET POTATO BISCUITS

ROAST THYME & CITRUS CHICKEN

MUSHROOM, GARLIC &
PARSLEY LASAGNA CUPCAKES

VIRGINIA FARMSTEAD CHEESE BAR

LOCALVORE LETTUCE WRAPS

ORGANIC BABY MIXED

☐ Plated Style

For this style dinner, members of the kitchen staff compose the individual plates for each course, and members of the waitstaff serve the plates individually to each guest. The price per guest of a plated dinner depends on the number of courses and the entrée(s) you decide to offer. You can splurge by offering multiple courses and/or showcasing the talents of a particular chef, or you can save money by focusing the meal on the choice of a savory entrée and offering a more simple first course.

☐ Small Plates Style

This tapas-style dinner features small composed plates, similar to mini-entrées, either served by members of the waitstaff carrying hawker trays or placed at food stations or on dining tables. Small plates dinners sometimes require extra kitchen staff and waitstaff to accommodate the time needed to compose all of the plates. On the plus side, small plates dinners allow for a large variety of food to be served and guests to enjoy dining at their own pace.

☐ Stations Style

For this style dinner, each station serves as a mini-buffet, featuring a grouping of foods that go well together. Stations provide a perfect way to showcase regional specialties, family recipes, and your personal preferences. If you decide to have a cocktail reception, consider adding select food stations.

Dessert Reception

A dessert reception, which usually follows an evening ceremony, features a variety of sweets and sometimes a small selection of savory foods. These parties generally last two to three hours and should begin late enough that guests do not expect dinner to be served (be sure to specify "desserts" on your wedding reception invitation so your guests can plan accordingly). This type of reception, like a brunch reception, can be more budget-friendly than a cocktail or dinner reception.

Choosing a Caterer

Regardless of the style reception you choose, you will probably want a professional caterer to help you make decisions about the foods and beverages, as well as handle most, if not all, of the venue setup, food preparation/presentation/serving, breakdown, and cleanup. Hotels and other banquet facilities generally require that you use their in-house (on-site) food services or a preselected exclusive caterer (preferred vendor). In general, hotels factor the food and beverage minimum investment into your contract for the venue so you will already know what to expect in terms of base pricing for the food services. In this situation, you don't have to spend time researching and choosing a caterer—so you can focus your efforts on personalizing the existing menu options, if they do not already meet your needs and wants. To avoid unexpected additional costs, refer to "Asking Questions about Catering Services" (page 210) to be sure that you have all the information you need before you make or request changes to the venue's existing catering packages.

If you are planning to have your reception at a private residence, historic property, or another venue that does not offer food services, you will need to find and hire an appropriate catering company. Just as you did when you planned the other elements of your wedding, sit down with your groom and family members and discuss your Buzz Words (page 14) and Inspiration Board (page 32). Reviewing your initial ideas about food items, specialty drinks, and the overall look and style you prefer will prepare you to describe your vision in detail to a caterer.

When you have a clear picture of what you want in mind, research the catering services in your area, and pay close attention to the types of events they handle, their particular style, their sample menu, and general pricing guidelines. Talk or meet with several of them, share your ideas, ask for information and suggestions, and request they send you a proposal. You want to choose a caterer who not only is

available on your wedding date, but who also understands your preferences, can help you bring your vision to life, and fits within your budget.

When you discuss your event with potential caterers, offer as much detail as you can so they can provide appropriate information about their services and how they can meet your specific wants and needs. This extra effort on your part will result in proposals that are more comparable to each other so you can make an informed choice.

Sharing Information with Potential Caterers

▪ The planned start and end times for your reception: _____
_____

▪ The overall look and style you want: _____
_____
_____

▪ Your food presentation and service style preferences: _____
_____
_____

▪ Must-have foods and beverages: _____
_____
_____

▪ Foods and beverages you do not want: _____
_____
_____

▪ Any religion-specific food requirements: _____
_____
_____

▪ The approximate number of expected guests and the number of people in your bridal party: _____
_____

▪ The amount you have budgeted for food, beverages, and catering services: _____

Asking Questions about Catering Services

The company:

☐ How long has the company been in business? _____

☐ Will the person you work with throughout the planning process be on-site the day of your wedding reception? _____

The food:

☐ What are their culinary strengths? _____

_____

☐ Where do their ingredients come from? _____

_____

☐ Are the foods cooked from scratch on-site, or are they prepared ahead of time and heated in warming drawers? _____

_____

☐ Are they willing to personalize the menu offerings to fit your tastes? _____

_____

☐ How do they accommodate special dietary needs? _____

_____

☐ Can they provide the wedding and groom's cakes? _____

_____

☐ When is the final guest count due? _____

☐ Do they provide on-site vendor meals? _____

☐ What happens to any leftover food? _____

_____

The food tasting:

☐ Do they offer a food tasting? _____

☐ Does it cost extra? _____

_____

☐ When and where will it be? _____

_____

☐ What happens during the tasting? _____

_____

☐ How many people are you allowed to bring with you? _____

The beverages:

☐ Do they have a liquor license? _____

☐ Are they prepared and willing to serve alcoholic beverages? _____

_____

☐ Are you allowed to provide some or all of the alcoholic beverages? _____

_____

Their services:

☐ What are their service strengths? _____

_____

☐ Have they worked in your venue? _____

☐ If your ceremony and reception are at the same venue, would they be willing to provide and set up chairs for the ceremony and perhaps provide pre-ceremony beverages? _____

_____

☐ What style(s) of food presentation and waitstaff service do they offer? _____

_____

☐ What is the ratio of servers to guests? _____

Rental equipment:

☐ Do they provide and/or coordinate any rental equipment? _____

_____

Pricing, fees, and taxes:

☐ Can they accommodate your budget? _____

☐ Is a minimum amount required? _____

_____

☐ Is there a fee to cut and serve the wedding cake(s)? _____

☐ What type of payment do they accept? _____

_____

☐ What are their delivery fees? _____

☐ What are their service fees? _____

_____

☐ What are the tax percentages? _____

■ **Contract and securing the date:**

☐ What are the steps to obtaining a proposal and securing the date? _____

_____

_____

_____

Evaluating Catering Proposals and Booking a Caterer

Do your homework, and evaluate the catering proposals you receive on more than just the bottom line. Staying within your budget is important, but be sure you are not sacrificing anything—including comfort and good service for your guests.

Questions	Caterer:	Caterer:	Caterer:
What do you think about the menus they selected for your reception?			
How many service staff will they provide?			
How much time did they budget for setup?			
What types and brands of beverages are they offering?			
Do they offer upgraded rental equipment or just a standard selection?			
What is their bottom-line estimate?			
Are they offering any incentives?			

Here are some helpful tips for meeting with and comparing caterers.

Connect with your catering representative. You should always feel like an important client when you are talking or meeting with your representative. If you choose this caterer, you will be working together constantly throughout the planning process, and this person will play a major role in executing your plans on your wedding day. Your representative should guide and educate you throughout the proposal process and help make you feel comfortable and secure with the choices you make.

Share your budget with your catering representative at your first meeting, and ask for a proposal that includes a few price points. This will ensure that you receive enough options to compare one caterer to another, as well as one menu to another.

Look for descriptions of where the food ingredients come from and how they are prepared, how the various dishes are displayed and served, and the kind of dining experience your guests will have.

Do not bargain hunt. It is fine to see if a potential caterer can match a competitor's pricing, but your final selection should not be decided by the company that gives you the most for free. Every product and service comes with a price tag, and your budget may not allow you to include everything on your wish list. When it comes to talking about the bottom line, some caterers may be more flexible on prices due to seasonal considerations or their schedule.

Don't always expect a food tasting before signing a contract. Some catering companies offer group informational tasting sessions, while others create a tasting for each client after they accept their proposal. You should be able to select your caterer based on reputation, reviews, and flexibility. Keep in mind that the catering proposal is just the guideline for your planning—a good caterer should be willing to revise the plan and adjust the menu until it fits your specific wants and needs. You will determine the final menu at the food tasting, which typically comes three to six months before your wedding date.

words of wisdom: Remember to ask each caterer to include estimates of all service fees and taxes in his or her proposals. "Plus service" and "plus tax" are usually additions to the final catering bill—having estimates of these costs in advance will help you stay within your budget.

Working with Your Caterer

This will likely be the first time you work with a catering manager on planning and executing a sizable, detail-oriented event. When you meet with the caterer you have hired or your venue's on-site or exclusive caterer, provide as much information as you can to help him or her succeed in meeting your expectations and fulfilling your vision for your reception. Also be sure to ask as many questions as necessary to make sure you fully understand the caterer's contract or proposal so you can work together to make any necessary changes.

JOAN'S
mint julep

4 parts bourbon whiskey
2 bunches fresh spearmint
1 part sparkling water
1 part sugar

mix & enjoy!

Here are some important issues to discuss with your caterer.

Staffing

Your catering team will be in charge of making sure your reception runs smoothly from start to finish. These professionals are trained to provide such a high level of excellence in food, beverage, and guest management that it almost appears as if they are anticipating your every need. As you read your caterer's proposal and/or contract, pay close attention to the number of service personnel and the cost— these amounts directly relate to the quality of service you will receive. Make sure you understand how many people will be handling each portion of your reception (setup, food preparation/presentation/ service, beverages, wedding and groom's cakes, breakdown, and cleanup) and what each member of the service team will be doing.

- ☐ Make sure there will be enough staff on-site to adequately meet the needs of your bridal party plus each of your guests. Think about when you eat at a restaurant—you might enjoy the most delicious food, but an overextended waiter will leave a bad taste in your mouth. That undesirable situation might easily become a reality at your reception if your caterer doesn't plan well.

- ☐ Remember the catering staff members who will be playing important roles behind the scenes. Your reception cannot run smoothly without the help of the on-site delivery truck drivers, setup and breakdown staff, and the culinary team. Respectfully accept your caterer's staffing guidelines for the number of people required to adequately handle all of these responsibilities.

- ☐ You don't need every catering staff member on-site for the entire reception, so for the most value—and to keep your reception budget in check—ask your caterer to stagger the arrival and departure times for the various staff members. The largest group of staff members should be at the venue from the setup through most of the food service; the dessert service, breakdown, and cleanup will usually go just fine with fewer hands on deck. Keep in mind, though, that your caterer may not be able to accommodate this request if you have a particularly short setup time or complicated food service logistics.

- ☐ A good rule of thumb is to plan for one waiter for every 10 guests and one bartender for every 40 guests.

Providing for Guests with Special Needs

Attending to any special needs your guests may have is your responsibility as the host of this special event. Accommodating guests who have specific dietary needs should be a priority, and you should include spaces on your reception invitation reply card for guests to indicate if they prefer a vegetarian or vegan meal, have any allergies, or if they have religion-specific dining preferences. Track these preferences and requirements, and give a list to your caterer.

Providing Meals for On-site Vendors

It is polite to offer a meal to vendors who will be on-site during the event. Read each vendor's contract carefully because some service providers require they be served a meal—sometimes a specific type of meal. Vendor meals may seem like just another added expense, but remember that these people will provide crucial services on your wedding day. Providing a meal is a gracious way to say "thank you" and acknowledge your appreciation of their time and talent.

The Food Tasting

The food tasting will be one of the more interesting and exciting appointments you and your groom will share during the planning process for your ceremony and reception. If the caterer did not provide a tasting before you hired him or her, schedule a tasting date and time immediately after you sign the contract. Plan to have the tasting close to the season in which your wedding will take place so the flavors of the ingredients will be as accurate as possible. If you plan to have a menu card printed, be sure to schedule the food tasting early enough to give you time to send the printer your final food selections.

Once the food tasting is scheduled, tell your caterer which items you and your groom would like to sample. Almost every catering company has its own procedures for the food tasting and making the final menu decisions—allow your caterer to guide you through the steps.

Here are some tips to help you make the food tasting a productive experience for you and your caterer:

- [ ] A food tasting is a fun occasion, but you should treat it like a business lunch with a clear agenda and definitive goals to accomplish.

- [ ] Ask your caterer in advance how many guests may join you. Just like shopping for your wedding dress, sometimes it is helpful to have fewer opinions.

- [ ] Discuss with your caterer ahead of time exactly what food items you want to taste, including any special requests.

- [ ] If your caterer is providing the alcoholic beverages for your reception, ask to taste the dinner wines or any specialty cocktails during the food tasting to make sure they meet your expectations.

- [ ] Plan to make decisions about the foods and beverages at the end of the tasting session—this is when you will best remember the taste of each item.

- [ ] Take photos of your final food selections so you remember the plating style and portion sizes—this will come in handy when you select the china and flatware to use at your reception.

- [ ] Make notes about what you like and don't like so you will remember why you chose certain items and rejected others.

- [ ] Don't be afraid to speak up if you do not like something. It is always easier to correct a problem in person rather than discuss it over the phone later.

- [ ] Use the downtime between courses to discuss the flow of the food service—this will help you determine the timeline for your reception.

- [ ] Give your caterer written feedback on your final food selections, and request an updated proposal that reflects any changes that were made during or immediately after the tasting.

Notes:

Reception Menu Planning

■ Style of Reception: _____

_____

_____

_____

_____

■ Number of Expected Guests: _____

_____

_____

_____

_____

■ Food Selection: _____

_____

_____

_____

_____

■ Special Stations: _____

_____

_____

_____

■ Beverages: _____

_____

_____

_____

_____

■ Cake Selection: _____

_____

_____

The Bar

A well-stocked bar is a must-have for many couples, and most guests will appreciate the opportunity to select their beverage of choice. Discuss the different options available with your caterer, and make sure you understand how the options will impact your budget and plans for your reception. If you are not allowed to provide your own alcoholic beverages, you will probably have two hosted bar options.

Libations

Courtney's Classic St. Germain Cocktail
Andy's Basil Gin Gimlet

Sauvignon Blanc
Pinot Grigio
Dry Chenin Blanc

Stella Artois
Pilsner Urquell
Paulaner Lager
Paulaner Hefeweizen

Assorted Non-Alcoh
fizzy drink
fresh iced

Consumption Bar Option

With a consumption bar, the host pays only for what is consumed measured by the glass or each opened bottle. This arrangement works well for a reception where the guests are light to moderate drinkers. If your caterer or venue offers this option, ask about how each drink is priced—mixed drinks with more than one kind of liquor usually cost more than a glass of wine or a beer.

An easy way to keep the final bill as low as possible is to offer a carefully edited bar selection. For example, instead of offering every kind of alcohol found in an open bar, you can select a few wines, a select group of micro brews, and two specialty cocktails, which gives guests a choice of beverages but still guides their decisions.

With an open bar, the host pays a flat per-person rate for the bar for the event. This option, which is usually available at different package price points, is based on the different kinds of alcoholic beverages being offered and the price level of different brands desired. Open bar packages generally cost more than consumption bar packages, but they allow flexibility in the beverages you offer and include a specialty cocktail at no extra cost. If you know that many of your guests will have more than two or three drinks, the open bar option may prove to be more affordable than a consumption bar.

Most caterers and venues that offer an open bar have two or three available packages.

☐ **House Package:** This level, which is the least expensive, offers less expensive brands of liquor and usually a limited selection of wine and beer.

☐ **Standard Package:** The next step up in cost, the standard package features recognizable name brands of liquor and a better selection of wine and beer.

☐ **Premium Package:** This is the most expensive package, and it features high-end liquors, a variety of well-curated wines and Champagne, and the best beers.

details, details, details

If you are planning to provide your own alcoholic beverages, ask your caterer for a breakdown of how much of each kind you should purchase. A basic "full bar" contains the following items.

❀ Champagne or Prosecco
❀ Red and white wine
❀ Beer and light beer
❀ Bourbon
❀ Gin
❀ Light Rum
❀ Scotch
❀ Tequila
❀ Vodka
❀ Dry and sweet vermouth
❀ Whiskey
❀ A variety of soft drinks, sparkling water, juices, and mixers

When discussing bar options with your caterer, don't forget to consider the following details:

☐ The amount you have budgeted for the bar.

☐ Does the caterer or venue hold the liquor license?

☐ If you are allowed and plan to provide your own alcoholic beverages, who will deliver them to the venue?

☐ Do you plan to offer a hosted bar for the entire reception or just the first hour or two?

☐ Are you planning to have a Champagne toast or serve wine with dinner? If you are serving wine with dinner, will the bar remain open during the meal?

☐ What liquor brands do you, your groom, your families, and your guests enjoy most?

☐ Are you planning to offer a specialty beverage or cocktail?

☐ Are bartenders included in your catering staff, or do you need to hire outside bartenders?

Rental Equipment

Tables, tablecloths, napkins, chairs, cushions, plates, glassware, and flatware are just some of the "basic" items you might need to rent so you and your guests will have a comfortable, enjoyable, gracious dining experience at your reception. Some venues have these items on-site. If your venue does not provide them, you will need to rent them through your caterer or on your own.

Tables

Rental tables come in a variety of sizes and shapes (see the chart below). When you are planning what tables to order, take into account the floor plan of the room and how many guests you need to seat. Sometimes, a classic arrangement of round tables accents the decor of a busy room, while other times mixed table shapes add interest to a predictable space. Most rental companies carry a variety of styles and coordinating linens.

Here is a guideline for how many guests each table size will typically accommodate and the size linen needed to cover each table to the floor.

Table size/shape	Seats	Linen size
2′ x 42″ cabaret	Tall cocktail	120″ round
3′ round	2-4	96″ round
4′ round	4-6	108″ round
5′ round	6-10	120″ round
5′ square	8	120″ x 120″ square
5′ 6″ round	8-10	126″ round
6′ round	10-12	132″ round
6′ square	8-12	132″ x 132″ square
6′ x 30″ rectangle	6	90″ x 132″
8′ x 30″ rectangle	6-8	90″ x 156″
8′ x 36″ x 30″ rectangle	6-8	96″ x 156″
8′ x 42″ x 30″ rectangle	8-10	102″ x 156″

Tablecloths

Tablecloths come in a wide array of prices, colors, and fabrics, ranging from moderately priced simple white cotton to expensive custom creations. Choose ones that enhance the color palette and overall look and style you have chosen for your special day—and that fit your budget.

Here are a few things to remember when you consider the available options.

■ **Tablecloths should always go to the floor.** No one wants to look at the less-than-attractive metal legs of a rental or banquet table. The only exception is to use a runner across the top of an attractive table.

■ **All of the tablecloths don't have to be the same.** Consider mixing complementary colors, patterns, and textures to not only create a custom look but also to prevent the room from appearing like "a sea of tables." This strategy can allow you to include some expensive linens in small quantities.

■ **Take the temperature of your environment into account.** If there is the chance that cold drinks might "sweat," pick tablecloths that will withstand the extra moisture. Very shiny satins and most silks water-spot easily.

■ **Remember tablecloths for the cocktail tables, bars, escort card table, and the cake tables.** These are perfect places to use accent colors and provide an unexpected pop of color, pattern, or texture without going overboard in the overall look or cost.

■ **Always order an extra of each size and color tablecloth in case one arrives damaged or spotted or an accident happens during setup.** It is a small price to pay to ensure the integrity of your overall look.

words of wisdom: For a streamlined, polished room setting, make sure the seams of the tablecloths all face the same direction. This small detail really does make a big difference in the overall appearance!

Napkins

Napkins offer a great way to add detail without necessarily incurring a huge expense, so consider personalizing and styling them to complement your overall look. Here are a few suggestions.

- Consider personalizing paper cocktail napkins and offering them with passed hors d'oeuvres, as well as on the bar(s) and at stations.

- Choose 5-inch cloth napkins with detailed stitching along the hemline for a classic, perfect look for a specialty beverage or cocktail plate.

- Transform basic cloth dinner napkins with an interesting pocket-style fold to hold the menu card and also accent each plate on the dining tables.

- Enhance your color palette by adding pops of color to the tablecloths with napkins.

- If you have time, make your own cloth napkins. Just cut 18- to 24-inch squares from a fabric that complements your color palette, and machine stitch a simple or decorative hem. As a personal thank-you gift, launder the napkins, and send them to special guests—but be sure to keep some for yourself and family members as keepsakes.

Chairs

Choose rental chairs that not only serve a functional purpose, but also enhance the overall look of the setting. Here are a few common styles to consider.

Ballroom/Banquet	metal frame, stacks easily, upholstered padded seat and back cushion	
Bellini	plastic, lightweight, thin modern design	
Bentwood	rounded back, looks like a bistro chair	
Chivari	the most common, more narrow than other options	
Folding	best for use in grass, usually the least expensive	
Ghost	Louis XV details, available with and without arms	
Ladderback	back support resembles a ladder	

China, Flatware, and Glassware

China

Ask your caterer or your chef about his or her preferred plate sizes and quantities, keeping in mind that the plate you select not only affects how the food looks when it is served, but also how much food will be served. Most chefs prefer a nice amount of "white space" on the plate.

Flatware

Choose flatware in a style and color that complements the china, glassware, tablecloths, chairs, and overall style of the room setting. Ask your caterer for the exact utensils and suggested quantities you should order.

Glassware

You will need to choose a variety of glassware for your reception. Before you select the styles to use, make a list of the beverages you are planning to offer. Also keep in mind the appropriate size of each glass—using a glass that is too large might result in the server filling it more than necessary, resulting in higher beverage costs and potentially more waste.

words of wisdom: To help keep the tables looking clean and uncluttered, forgo using bread and butter plates. Instead, ask your caterer to have waitstaff butler the bread from a tray or basket when the first course is served, offering it to each guest individually and placing it on the first course plate.

☐ 1. Base plate: 12"–13"

☐ 2. Dinner plate: 10"–11"

☐ 3. Salad (or dessert) plate: 8"– 9"

☐ 4. Bread plate

☐ 5. Bread knife

☐ 6. Salad fork

☐ 7. Dinner fork

☐ 8. Dinner knife

☐ 9. Salad knife

☐ 10. Dessert spoon and fork

Your caterer can guide you on what kind and how many of each glass to order.

Glass	Good for:	Quantity ordered:
Wine	Cocktail and dinner wines	
Flute	Champagne, sparkling drinks	
Rocks	Mixed drinks, single pours	
Collins/Highball	Non-alcoholic drinks, classic mixed cocktails	
Pilsner	Beer	
Martini	Martini drinks	
All-Purpose	Non-alcoholic drinks, beer, mixed cocktails	

Platters and Plates for Buffets and Food Stations

Long gone are the days of silver chafing dishes and billowing fabric on buffet and food station tables. So consult with your caterer about the appropriate serving platters and cocktail or dinner plates to order if you are planning a buffet or food stations. Here are a few things to consider and discuss to help make sure your food displays look styled and complement your overall look.

How many tables or displays are needed so guests do not have to wait in long lines?

■ Think about function: Hot foods should be served hot, and cold foods should be kept cold. In addition, foods should look and taste fresh—no one likes eating a meal that has been sitting out for an extended period of time.

■ If you are not providing a menu card at each dining table or guest's place setting, consider using a large menu board or individual labels for each food item. This will alert guests who have food allergies or dietary requirements and help them make appropriate choices.

■ Select appropriate weight and size dinner plates—they should be light enough for guests to carry easily and hold a normal serving of food.

■ Where will flatware be available? If it will be too cumbersome for guests to carry flatware along with plates of food, consider arranging it on the table rather than at the buffet or food stations. Also consider how the flatware will be presented or displayed.

■ Work together with your caterer on the food service timeline. Keep in mind that not every station needs to be "open" at the same time. For a cocktail reception, consider rotating the opening of the individual stations to keep guests moving about the room.

■ To help manage lines if you are planning a buffet, arrange to have the waitstaff prompt the guests at each table when it is their turn to fill their plates.

Planning and Booking Music Entertainment

Some of the most important and fun decisions you will make involve choosing the music that will fill the air at your reception and help create the mood and energy you want for this special time. As with every aspect of your wedding day, the soundtrack should be a reflection of you and your groom.

Start with your Buzz Words (page 14) and imagine the kind of music that will enhance and evoke the mood of the party you envision. If your reception is a formal, black-tie affair, consider hiring a full band capable of playing a broad selection of dance music. If you are having an intimate, laid-back barbeque dinner reception at your parents' home, you may want a bluegrass band to highlight the casual ambience.

Consider the following questions when you start planning the musical entertainment for your reception.

■ How much does your budget allow for music entertainment? _____
_____
_____

■ Do your guests enjoy dancing, or are they more into just talking and mingling with one another? _____
_____
_____

■ Will you need music to cover multiple events (such as a cocktail hour, the reception, and an after-reception party) and perhaps even multiple locations? _____
_____
_____

■ If your ceremony and wedding reception are at the same venue, does it make sense to have the same group or select musicians from a band provide both the ceremony and cocktail hour music?
_____
_____

■ What are the logistical constraints of your reception venue? Is there space for a band, or would a DJ be a better fit? _____
_____
_____

■ How many instruments and vocalists do the bands you are considering offer? _____
_____
_____

■ Do you like a majority of the music they perform on their list of sample songs? _____
_____
_____

Selecting and Booking a Band

From classical string groups, band orchestras, and upbeat dance bands to country groups and cover bands, live music can create not only ambience but also visual impact. Ask local wedding and event planners and look in local publications for recommendations. Also contact local talent companies that represent music groups—these agencies typically book a diverse array of musical talent and can tell you about each group, their availability, and pricing.

Bands often have a list of requirements for you as well, known as a "rider." These can range from spatial requirements to meal preferences. Be sure to ask the band or their booking agent to disclose these to you before you sign a contract with the group.

Booking your band will include a contract stating the hours they are agreeing to perform for your wedding and the pieces (instruments) and number of members you are booking. The contract should also include how the group handles substitutions if a member is unable to perform at your wedding for any reason. Bands usually require a deposit up front when you book them, with the balance due on or before your wedding date.

Ask these questions when hiring a musical group.

Questions	Band Name:	Band Name:	Band Name:
How many pieces does the band offer? Are additional pieces available? How much does it cost to add pieces?			
Can you have a full list of songs the band knows? Will the band work with you on playlists?			
Can the band provide you with a sample song list from another wedding so you can see what types of songs they played and the order?			
Are they willing to learn a new song or two if you have something specific they do not currently list in their repertoire?			
Does the band play sample showcases that are open to the public? If not, is there any opportunity for you to see the band perform live before you book them?			
Does the band have a Web site that includes videos of live performances? Or can the band provide you with a promotional video?			
Is the group local, or will you also have to pay travel fees?			
Can one of the vocalists act as an emcee when needed? Is their speaking demeanor appropriate?			
Do they play any special songs you know you will need, like the Hora?			
Do they provide music when they take a break? Or do you have to provide the break music?			
What do they wear when they perform?			
Can they provide references from several previous wedding clients?			

Selecting and Booking a DJ

Hiring a DJ can be more economical than hiring a band. In addition, a DJ will have much more versatility, because he has access to just about any song or group you would want to hear. Also, DJs are able to smoothly transition from song to song and keep the momentum constant because they do not take the defined breaks a band takes.

Because a DJ will also serve as an emcee at your reception, be sure you are comfortable with his personality and demeanor. Also discuss your expectations about how much (or little) you want him to talk, and give him a script to use when introducing speakers or making announcements to help avoid any unwanted or inappropriate wording.

Prior to signing a contract with a DJ, be sure you understand how a substitution will be handled if he is unable to perform for any reason. DJs usually require a deposit due at booking, with the balance due on or before your wedding date.

Ask these questions of DJs you are considering.

Questions	DJ Name:	DJ Name:	DJ Name:
Can you have a full list of songs he/she has? Will the DJ work with you on playlists?			
Can he/she provide you with a sample song list from a previous wedding so you can see what types of songs he/she plays and the order?			
Will he/she let you give them music they might not have that you want to have played?			
What does he/she wear when he/she performs?			
Is his/her equipment compact or more elaborate?			
Can you get several past wedding client references to contact?			

Musical Group Requirements

Your band or DJ will have specific requirements for you and your reception venue. Be sure you understand and clarify these requirements so there are no surprises on your wedding day that might impact their ability to set up or even perform. These requirements can include but are not limited to the following.

- **Setup Time:** How much time do they require for setup? Does this work with the amount of setup time your venue allows you to have?

- **Space:** How much physical space do they require? Is the room able to accommodate their space requirements with your anticipated guest count?

- **Build-out Requirements:** Do they require you to provide a stage? Lighting? Tables?

- **Power:** How many plugs and amps do they require? What is the distance between the power source and where the band will be located? Can the venue support these requirements without risking blowing a fuse? If you are in an outside venue space, where will power come from? Who will provide the generator if needed?

- **Loading In/Out:** Are they able to get to and from the reception space from the designated unloading areas?

- **Breaks:** How many breaks will they take? How long are the breaks? Do they require a greenroom for breaks or changing?

- **Meals:** How many meals will you need to provide for members and any technical or sound staff? Usually you will not need to include these meals in your guest count, and your caterer can provide a vendor meal for each of the group members you are responsible to feed.

- **Other:** Do they require any other specific items such as parking or bottled water in their greenroom?

Making Your Music Playlist

At least one month prior to your wedding date, you and your groom should finalize your music selections and give your list to your band or DJ. Also notify them of songs or types of music you absolutely do not want to hear or have played at your wedding. Discuss with them what songs you want to be played during dinner, when things should be generally low key, and when they should kick off any high-energy dance sets.

Give clear direction to your band or DJ about your selections for the bride and groom and bridal party introductions, your first dance as a married couple, your father/daughter dance, your mother/son dance, the cake-cutting ceremony, and the last song of the evening. Be sure you give the specific version of each song, including any group that might have performed the song if it is not the original version, to avoid any miscommunication.

If you do not have strong feelings about a specific song for one of your special dances, ask your band or DJ to suggest songs they have played for those dances. If you select a song that is a tad longer than you would like to be out on the dance floor as the center of attention, be sure to discuss ways the band or DJ can shorten it.

Wedding Playlist

_____   _____
_____   _____
_____   _____
_____   _____
_____   _____
_____   _____
_____   _____
_____   _____
_____   _____
_____   _____
_____   _____
_____   _____
_____   _____
_____   _____
_____   _____
_____   _____
_____   _____

words of wisdom: Consider and discuss with your band or DJ how you want them to handle any song requests made by guests during your reception. Often couples decide they want to retain control over the music selections and do not allow the band or DJ to play requested songs they have not approved. The same consideration should be made for any impromptu speaking requests made by guests—it's not a good idea to turn the microphone over to someone who might cause embarrassment or create an uncomfortable situation.

Indoor Space Planning Checklist

Having your reception in an indoor space does provide a sense of relief from any weather-related worries, but you will still have some logistical concerns. Here are general questions to ask and considerations to cover when you are finalizing your plans. You can also use this list to double-check your plans during your final walk-through.

☐ *How much time will vendors have on the front end for setting up? How much time will vendors have at the end of your reception for breakdown and cleanup?*

☐ *If you are bringing in an outside caterer, be sure your venue contact explains where the kitchen areas are located or can be placed and any policies they might have on serving and cooking inside.*

☐ *What special instructions should be provided to all of your reception vendors for delivery times and unloading/loading areas? Does the route to the reception space require the use of elevators or include long walks down hallways? Be sure you set up your vendors for success if they have not done a wedding at the venue so they are not surprised by any logistical hiccups.*

☐ *Will your venue representative be touching base with your caterer, florist, music contact, and other vendors prior to your wedding date to go over policies and instructions on working within the venue space? Discuss with your venue representative any requirements from your vendors, such as where the band can take breaks and where the cake will be stored when the baker delivers it.*

☐ *What are the power limitations (if any) in the room for music and lighting? Be sure you discuss the needs of your band or DJ with your venue representative in advance.*

☐ *Does the venue or room include a dance floor, tables, and/or chairs? Can some or all of the furniture or other pieces be removed prior to the wedding?*

☐ *Discuss with your caterer and venue representative what the space setup will look like for dinner tables, bars, musical entertainment, and any other necessary furniture and equipment. Be sure there is enough space to accommodate the number of people, furniture, and* equipment you are planning for, and create an accurate, to-scale floor plan to show the placement of all of the pieces.

☐ What is lighting like in the room? Is the house lighting on dimmers? Can the house lighting alone provide the atmosphere you want to achieve in the room? Ask your venue representative to show you how the room will look with the available lighting.

☐ Do you need to consider bringing in a professional lighting company to place perimeter uplighting, pin-spotting for dinner tables, or highlighting for the dance floor or band?

☐ How is the temperature in the room controlled? Does it have heat and/or air-conditioning? If not, what might you need to consider if the weather conditions are less than ideal and comfortable for guests? Can you bring in heaters? Can you bring in fans?

☐ What is the parking situation? To avoid any unpleasant or embarrassing surprises, be sure to find out what parking is allowed, if any, and any costs for parking the venue might charge your guests. If necessary, offer to pay and validate parking for your guests. If a permit is required for street parking, work with your venue representative to find out how you can reserve spaces if necessary. If street parking is not available, consider hiring a valet company to give your guests an easy option for getting to and from your reception.

☐ Are you able to drop off any items for storage prior to your wedding date?

☐ What designated date and time can you have for the rehearsal practice if you are having your ceremony at the venue?

☐ Is there a designated coat check area? Does the venue supply coat check attendants, or do you need the caterer to provide staff?

☐ How many restrooms are accessible to guests? Are there enough to meet your guests' needs? Who is responsible for refreshing them? Can you place flowers, toiletries, or decorative items in the restrooms?

☐ What are the policies on decorations? Can you hang or rig items from the ceiling? Are there hooks already in place? Can you hang anything from the walls? What are the rules on other areas you think you might like to decorate, such as mantels, front steps, or existing furniture? Do they allow candles to be lighted on dinner tables and any other specific spaces? Do candles have to have a contained flame?

Notes:_____

Notes: _____

_____

_____

_____

_____

_____

_____

_____

_____

_____

_____

_____

_____

_____

_____

_____

_____

_____

_____

_____

_____

_____

_____

_____

_____

_____

_____

_____

Outdoor Space Planning Checklist

Creating a wedding in an outside space can be a beautiful opportunity to take advantage of scenic views or lush garden spaces. Planning for the worst-case weather scenario, however, is a MUST for peace of mind. If your venue has a permanent covered outdoor structure or tent already as part of the space and they regularly hold weddings here, some of these items on the checklist below might not apply, but they are all still important points to consider.

Here are general questions to ask and items to cover when you are finalizing your plans. You can also use this list to double-check your plans during your final walk-through.

☐ *What is your backup plan for a lightning storm, rain, wind, or unexpected cold or hot weather for any of your events? Is there an inside space available on the property that can accommodate all of your guests and events? Will guests be able to get to and from different parts of the property without getting soaked if it happens to be raining? What does your venue recommend as a "Plan B" if you are not able to hold the event outside?*

☐ *If you are planning to have a portion of your wedding, such as the ceremony, outside and the reception inside a tent, consider what the logistical constraints will be if you have to move the ceremony under the tent. Will the catering staff be able to "flip" the room easily from the ceremony to the reception? How distracting will this be to your guests? Where will the guests go while this is taking place?*

☐ *If you have to provide the tent, does your venue have a specific tent vendor you must work with?*

☐ *What are the policies, designated areas, and grounds-keeping rules related to installing a tent? Does the venue have diagrams of the space and terrain available that you can give to your tent vendor?*

☐ *How much time will vendors have on the front end for setting up? How much time will vendors have at the end of the evening for breakdown and cleanup?*

☐ *Where will the designated kitchen area be? Will you need to provide a second tent as a field kitchen for your caterer? If so, what size kitchen tent will they need? Will you need to connect the two tents so inclement weather will not disrupt food service? What other components are needed to build a kitchen, and are you responsible for the cost?*

☐ *Where will power come from? Is there an existing source already on the property that can accommodate all of the power needed for the reception tent, lighting, heating, fans, musical equipment, and catering kitchen?*

☐ *Will you need to provide a generator to run all of the power into the space? How much power will the generator need? Where will it be placed so it's hidden from view and the noise does not distract your guests? How much cabling and how many power cords will the vendors need to bring with them to connect to the generator from inside the tent?*

☐ *What special instructions do each of your wedding vendors need about delivery times and unloading/loading areas? Will they be able to pull trucks right up to the outside area? Is it a difficult route or terrain for equipment on rolling wheels or especially heavy items? Be sure you set up your vendors for success if they have not done a reception at your venue so they are not surprised by any problems that could delay and impact your wedding day schedule.*

☐ *Will your venue representative be touching base with your caterer, tent company, florist, music contact, and other vendors prior to your wedding date to go over their policies and instructions on working at the venue?*

☐ *Discuss with your tent company, caterer, and venue representative what the tent layout will look like, and design a floor plan that allows enough room for a dance floor, band or DJ space, all of the dinner tables, bars, and any other necessary furniture and equipment. Be sure there is enough room so that all of the areas can be completely under the tent, and be sure you have booked the proper size tent.*

☐ *What is lighting like in the tent? Is the lighting on dimmers? Who will be responsible for adjusting and lowering the lights during your reception?*

Notes:_____

Notes:_____
_____
_____
_____
_____
_____
_____
_____
_____
_____
_____
_____
_____
_____
_____
_____
_____
_____
_____
_____
_____
_____
_____
_____
_____
_____
_____
_____
_____
_____
_____
_____

☐ *Will the tent company provide lighting, or do you need to consider bringing in a professional lighting company to place tent lighting, perimeter uplighting, pin-spotting for dinner tables, or highlighting for the dance floor or band?*

☐ *What is lighting like around the outside property? Will guests be able to walk to and from spots on the property such as the entrance, exit, and restrooms safely? Do you need to install lighting along any walking paths?*

☐ *What are potential solutions to any temperature concerns? Do you need to have walls provided on the tent? Heater(s)? Fan(s)? Air-conditioning? How will these items be properly powered?*

☐ *How many restrooms are accessible to guests? Are there enough to meet your guests' needs?*

☐ *If restrooms are not available on the property and you must rent trailers, consider the distance and where it makes the most sense to place them so they are not a complete eyesore. Find out from the company providing the trailers what is needed to have them up and running properly. Where are the power and water sources?*

☐ *What is the parking situation? Be sure to understand what parking is allowed, as well as the safety and ease of walking for your guests. Consider hiring a valet company to give your guests an easy option for getting to and from your reception if self-parking is not optimal.*

☐ *What designated date and time can you have for the rehearsal if you are having your ceremony at the venue?*

☐ *What are the policies about decorations around the property and inside the tent? Can you hang or rig items from the tent ceiling or sides? What is the rule for other spaces you would like to decorate? Do they allow candles to be lighted on dinner tables and any other specific spaces you are interested in illuminating, or do the candles have to have a contained flame? Are there specific rules during dry-weather months when the risk of fire is greater?*

☐ *If you plan to do a send-off at the end of your reception, are there any limitations? Ask your venue representative to recommend where this should take place if there are multiple entrances/exits at the venue.*

Tents

If you need a tent for an outside space, you have many options and types of tent looks to consider. Since this space will essentially be the canvas of the room you are creating, go back to your Buzz Words (page 14) and Inspiration Board pictures (page 32) to determine what look you want for the tented area. Do you want a sailcloth tent with beautiful peaks and wood beam poles—or are you okay with a plastic tent and metal poles? Do you prefer a total "open air" experience and want a tent with clear ceiling and sides?

The tent company will work with you to determine the appropriate size tent you need based on your guest count and estimated table count, the size of your dance floor, the amount of space your music group requires, and the space you need for bars, cocktail hour, and any lounge settings. Talk with them about available options for lighting, heating, cooling, dance floors, and power. Typically tent vendors can supply and handle the generator for the tent, as well as the power requirements of your other vendors.

Ask the tent company to include options in your proposal about adding side walls, heaters, and fans, if they are needed. Be sure to find out what the deadline would be to add these items.

words of wisdom: Before you start to research tent companies, first ask your venue representative about the policies for tenting and if you must use a designated tent company. The tenting vendor will have to ask your venue representative about required permits. City, county, and state safety, fire code, and flame-resistant policies vary widely.

Enhancing Your Venue

Consider ways you can enhance key spaces at your reception venue without spending more than your budget will allow. Choose spots where your guests will appreciate the impact and wow factor of a special touch that complements your overall look and style. For instance, have an eye-catching floral arrangement created just for a driveway or front door, or place beautiful candlelit lanterns on the steps or walkway leading inside the building.

Lighting

Lighting affects the ambience and mood of a room, and it provides easy ways for you to highlight focal points and disguise less-attractive details. A decorator, interior designer, event planner, or other lighting professional can help you evaluate the existing lighting elements at your venue and offer suggestions to make the space appear more pleasing.

Here are some tips.

Call in a professional consultant. Ask your caterer or venue representative to recommend a professional, and arrange for him or her to do a walk-through with you. Point out the specific things you like about the venue spaces and the specific things you don't like, and ask the professional to propose a lighting plan that will meet your wishes and needs. When the plan is ready, meet with the professional to make sure you fully understand it.

Talk color. To help your professional consultant recommend appropriate lighting colors, show him or her swatches of the table linens you have chosen. Different lighting techniques can change the appearance of some fabrics and colors. For example, some shades of blue and purple look darker than usual, shades of red and orange appear more brown than usual, and bright whites do not look as crisp if they are not lit properly.

Lights out! Start in a dark room, and determine first what basic lighting elements you need to function. Then decide what architectural details or spaces you want to highlight in the room. Also decide what kind of lighting you need to create the mood you want.

Consider your photographer's needs. You need appropriate lighting for good-quality photographs. Ask your photographer for his or her preferences, and share these with your consultant so they can be included in the lighting plan. Keep in mind that saturated, brightly colored "party lighting" looks great in person, but you don't want purple- or blue-hued photographs in your wedding album.

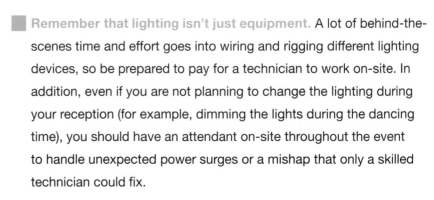

Remember that lighting isn't just equipment. A lot of behind-the-scenes time and effort goes into wiring and rigging different lighting devices, so be prepared to pay for a technician to work on-site. In addition, even if you are not planning to change the lighting during your reception (for example, dimming the lights during the dancing time), you should have an attendant on-site throughout the event to handle unexpected power surges or a mishap that only a skilled technician could fix.

Ask for pictures. To make sure that you completely understand your professional's lighting plan, ask him or her to provide pictures of the kind of fixtures and other elements.

words of wisdom : A gobo light adds pattern and texture to the area it is lighting. Consider using a subtle patterned gobo projected onto the dance floor to enhance the ambience and create a special look at your reception.

Specialty Furniture

You may want to consider using lounge or other specialty furniture pieces to create the setting you envision for your reception. Lounge furniture, which perhaps is the most common "specialty" rental item, includes couches, chaise lounge beds, oversize ottomans, and low accent tables. These pieces are commonly used with cafe seating in a cocktail area or around the dance floor to provide a place for guests to sit and mingle. Due to their large scale and bulkier weight, these furniture pieces often come with a large delivery fee and potentially a setup charge. Lounge furniture extends beyond the basic rental items you need for your reception, and these specialty items might not fit in your budget. If your Buzz Words (page 14) or Inspiration Board (page 32) include specialty rental items as a focal point in creating a specific environment (like a cocktail reception), plan in advance and choose these furniture pieces wisely.

Dance Flooring

The dance floor will be a popular spot during your reception. It will be the first place you and your husband share a dance, and it will appear in many treasured photographs.

Consider the style: Dance floors come in a variety of colors and fabrications. You can choose to either have your dance floor blend in with the rest of the setting or stand out as a focal point.

Think about shape: Not all dance floors are square. A rectangular floor might work better for your venue.

Location: The placement of the dance floor will impact the atmosphere of your reception. Remember that your band or DJ needs a flat, hard surface for their equipment. Plan to leave enough space for them plus a bit extra around them so your guests are not too close to the speakers. If your reception is in a tent with grass underfoot and you are not planning to put your band or DJ on a stage or platform, consider extending the dance floor so they can set up on it.

Size: Plan for 2 to 2.5 square feet per person. It is better to have the dance floor appear too full than empty. Dance flooring usually comes in 3- or 4-foot sections so your dimensions don't have to be exact.

Number of Guests	Suggested size (based on 2.5 sq/ft per guest)
50	12' x 12'
100	15' x 15'
150	18' x 18'
200	20' x 20'
250	24' x 24'
300	26' x 26'
350+	28' x 28' +

make it yours

Does your reception venue have ugly carpet? Before you panic, consider your floor plan. The carpet will disappear once the tables and chairs cover the floor and the appropriate lighting schematic is installed.

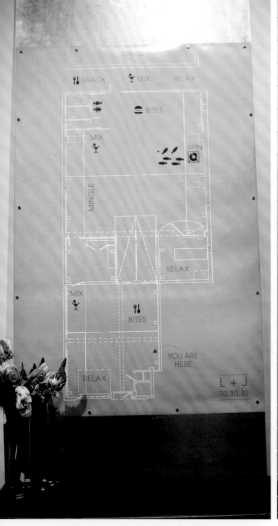

Designing a Floor Plan

Even if you are not a skilled draftsman, draw a floor plan so you can plan for and share with vendors how you want the reception venue room to look. Your caterer and/or venue representative might be able to produce a floor plan for you or, at the very least, give you the room dimensions. You can also easily create a floor plan in Word, Excel, or by hand.

Include the following details on your floor plan.

- The desired entrance and exit points

- Where the band or DJ will be placed and any necessary staging components

- The dance floor area

- How the dinner tables will be arranged and numbered

- Where the bar(s) will be placed

- Where other furniture settings, such as wedding and groom's cake display tables, cocktail tables and seating, escort card display table, dessert displays, and guest book table, will be placed

Sample Floor Plan

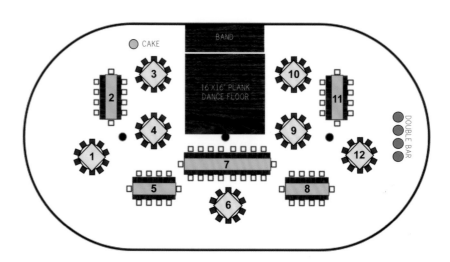

Organizing for Success

To help ensure that all of the details you have so carefully planned, designed, produced, and purchased are incorporated into your wedding just as you envisioned, be sure to organize, pack, and deliver items in a way that they can be easily found.

- Pack items in plastic storage containers with lids rather than boxes. The handles make the containers easy to lift, and you do not have to worry about packing tape, box cutters, water damage, etc. Use clear plastic containers whenever you can to help minimize the need to open the lid to see what's inside.

- Organize and pack items by the location where they will be used (for example, bridal party table, buffet, etc.). This will help the people setting up know exactly where each item goes.

- Pack all the paper products for each table together in one resealable plastic bag. Label each bag with the table number, and include the correct number of menus, place cards in order (if they are being used), and favors, plus a seating chart/list of guests at the table. Put all of the bags, in order of table number, in a plastic storage container for transport to your reception venue.

- If you want items styled in a specific way, do a mock-up at home and include a picture and instructions in the container with the items.

- Pack each item ready to put in its place. Before packing, remove all of the labels, price tags, and excess shipping/packaging material, and place candles either in their candleholders (if they won't get broken in transport) or with their candleholders. Don't rely on your catering staff or another on-site person to do these preproduction tasks for you during the precious, already busy setup time.

■ Number each of the containers, and make a list of what items are in each container. Give copies of the list to your catering manager and anyone else who is overseeing the setup so they can easily find items that need to be assembled or put in place first.

■ Prepare a "styling and emergency box" that includes all of the tools and supplies needed for any items that require assembly. Also include any emergency items that might be needed. Here are some suggestions, but feel free to add others—it is always better to be over-prepared.

- ☐ aspirin
- ☐ bandages and other basic first-aid supplies
- ☐ bobby pins
- ☐ box cutter and/or scissors
- ☐ double-sided tape
- ☐ extra votive and other candles
- ☐ glass cleaner
- ☐ glue
- ☐ heavy-duty extension cords
- ☐ iron
- ☐ lighters
- ☐ packing tape
- ☐ paper towels
- ☐ pens and fine-line markers that match your calligraphy color
- ☐ safety and straight pins
- ☐ trash bags
- ☐ zip ties

Giving Your Guests a Southern Welcome

Treating your guests graciously will make them feel welcomed and help them relax so they will be ready to fully enjoy being with you for your celebration. From arranging convenient, economical accommodations and leaving personalized welcome packages in their rooms to planning transportation to and from your ceremony and reception venues, you'll ensure that everyone will greatly appreciate the time and effort you put into meeting their needs.

Arranging Appropriate Accommodations

Once you have set your wedding date, booked the venues for your ceremony and reception, and compiled your guest list, start thinking about reserving rooms for people who live out of town. First, tally how many of your guests will probably need accommodations, and consider reserving blocks of rooms in nearby hotels, motels, and/or bed-and-breakfast establishments.

When you are determining the number of rooms to reserve, carefully consider all of the extenuating factors: Is your wedding in a destination location where everyone—you and your family, your groom and his family, all the members of your bridal party, plus all of your guests—will need accommodations? Is your wedding on a popular vacation or holiday weekend or in a busy city where rooms might book quickly?

Here are some tips on reserving blocks of rooms.

- Contact the hotel's or motel's group sales department or the bed-and-breakfast's owner or manager to ask about and arrange reserving blocks of rooms.

- Most hotels offer a discounted room rate if you reserve a block of 10 or more rooms.

- Reservation policies vary, but most hotels offer to hold a specific number of rooms that your guests can individually call to reserve. Your contract with the hotel, motel, or bed-and-breakfast for a block of rooms will probably include a deadline several weeks before the reservation date when the discounted rate will expire and any unbooked rooms will be released. Encourage your guests to reserve their rooms as soon as possible.

- The hotel, motel, or bed-and-breakfast will provide you with an event code name, which typically will be a combination of your last names (for example, "The Smith-Lee wedding"). Your guests will need to refer to this code when they call to reserve their rooms at the negotiated special rate.

make it yours

If your wedding is taking place at a hotel or bed-and-breakfast, be sure to ask about and research the advantages and discounts of reserving or "buying out" rooms at the location. Reserving all of the rooms at a smaller venue can create a sense of privacy and exclusivity for your guests.

- Be sure to give the specific details about the hotel, motel, or bed-and-breakfast where you have reserved a block of rooms on your wedding Web site and a wedding invitation insert. Include the special room rate, the deadline for reserving rooms at the special rate, and the event code name.

- Consider arranging blocks of rooms at two or more venues at different price point levels to give guests cost options.

- If any of the venues require you to sign a contract and make a financial commitment when you reserve a block of rooms, be conservative with the estimated number of the rooms you need—you don't want to be responsible for paying for any rooms that are not booked.

Hotel Name	Reservations Phone Number	Room Block Rate	Event Code Name	Reservation Deadline

Welcoming Your Guests to Their Rooms

Welcoming your guests to their rooms with a handwritten personal note and/or a thoughtful gift bag will let them know how much you appreciate their traveling to be with you on your special day. If you want the hotel, motel, or bed-and-breakfast staff to hand your guests a note or place a gift bag in their rooms, be sure to make those arrangements in advance—some venues provide this service free, while others charge per gift or room.

Guest Name	Hotel	Hotel location/ phone number	Date of Arrival	Date gift basket left

Try these ideas for welcome gifts.

- A personal note from you and your groom, along with a detailed schedule of the ceremony, reception, and any other wedding-related events; the address, phone number, and directions to each venue; a map of the area, including all your wedding event venues, places you recommend seeing, and your suggested favorite dining options; and any other fun details or tips you might want to give your guests

- Water bottles

- Sweet and savory snacks; regional snacks or ones that you and/or your groom especially like

- Aspirin, sunscreen, insect repellent, and other appropriate sundries

words of wisdom: Be smart on the packaging for your gift bags and don't think only pretty—also think practical. Make it easy for your guests by using a convenient bag that can either lie flat or easily fit in their luggage.

Who Hosts?

❧ Traditionally the bride and her mother host the bridesmaid luncheon.

❧ Traditionally the groom's parents host the rehearsal dinner and include immediate family members and the bridal party, as well as special and out-of-town guests.

❧ Traditionally the bride's parents host the post-wedding brunch and invite all of the wedding guests.

Including Your Guests at Additional Wedding-related Events

A welcome reception, farewell brunch, and/or other wedding-related parties can provide memorable opportunities for you to spend additional time with your family and friends. After you have booked the venues for your ceremony and reception and have set the schedule for your wedding day, begin considering any other events or activities you would like to enjoy with your guests.

Be sure to keep your wedding schedule and budget in mind when you plan these extras. Also carefully consider the following questions.

☐ Who will host and pay for each additional event or activity?

☐ For your bridesmaid luncheon (traditionally hosted by the bride and her mother) and rehearsal dinner (traditionally hosted by the groom's family), do you want to limit the invitation list to immediate family members and the bridal party—or do you want to include some special guests?

☐ If you are planning a welcome reception, farewell brunch, and similar parties, will your budget allow you to extend invitations to all of your wedding guests?

☐ Do you want to include the invitation to additional events as an insert in your wedding invitation—or do you want to send separate invitations?

If it is appropriate, add details about these additional events on your wedding Web site.

Accommodating Older Guests and Children

Keep in mind any special needs of the older and younger people on your guest list. To help ensure that everyone has an enjoyable time, plan ways to provide assistance and extra comfort for older guests who might have a difficult time getting around, and a special place plus age-appropriate, simple, nondisruptive activities to keep children happily entertained.

words of wisdom: Keep small guests entertained at your reception and other parties by creating a special "corner" where they can sit with other children. Decorate each table with a fun centerpiece they will enjoy, and provide crayons (avoid markers that can stain clothing), paper, and simple games. Ask your caterer to provide a child-friendly meal option, and serve children as soon as adult guests are seated for brunch, lunch, or dinner.

Providing Thank-you Favors

Saying thank-you to your guests with a small gift from you and your groom is a tradition that dates back centuries. Although providing a take-home gift is a nice gesture, it is not a requirement or necessity, and your guests will not notice if you don't give one. If your budget does allow it, consider giving a small item that will satisfy the majority of your guests. You can also use this opportunity to continue personalizing your wedding by packaging your favors in the color palette and style of the paper goods you have chosen for your special day.

Consider placing a favor at each place setting or display the favors on a special table where guests can pick up one as they leave your reception or another wedding-related party.

Here are some ideas to consider for favors.

- A traditional boxed chocolate, gourmet candy, or special local or regional treat
- Homemade preserves or cookies made from a favorite family recipe
- Flip-flops or other comfortable slip-on shoes to wear during or after dancing, or a pashmina or other simple wrap for a chilly evening at an outside reception
- Cookies, doughnuts, hot cocoa mix, and other mini desserts packaged "to go"

make it yours

In lieu of spending money on favors, consider making a donation in honor of your guests to a charity that is important to you and your groom.

Arranging Transportation

To help make sure that your wedding day flows as smoothly as possible and everyone arrives on time at your ceremony and reception venues, consider arranging transportation—especially if the travel distances are significant, traffic might be heavy, and adequate suitable parking will not be readily available. Your primary concern will be providing transportation for you and your family and your groom and his family, but as a courtesy also consider making arrangements for your bridal party and guests.

Research available transportation companies, and get pricing proposals from at least two that have earned reputations for providing reliable, courteous service with well-maintained vehicles driven by responsible drivers who can get everyone from point A to point B in a timely manner. Talk with the booking representative for each company about the most efficient and economical options for the type and size vehicles needed for your group and the planned routes and timing for picking up and delivering your guests. If your wedding venues and guest accommodations are a relatively short distance apart, consider using fewer vehicles and having them make "loops" to pick up and deliver groups of guests.

When you choose and book your transportation company, you will probably have to place a deposit to hold the vehicles you are planning to use. Be sure to ask the booking representative about the company's policies and deadlines for increasing or decreasing the number of vehicles in case your needs change as you get closer to your wedding date and have a better idea of your final number of guests. Most companies require that you book vehicles and drivers for a minimum number of consecutive hours, so do not be surprised if you have to pay for unused hours.

words of wisdom:

If your wedding venues are in a destination location or the closest airport is a significant distance away, consider arranging for shuttle service to the hotels, motels, and/or bed-and-breakfasts where your guests will be staying. If you are not arranging transportation, be sure to give your guests information about available airport shuttle service or car rental options.

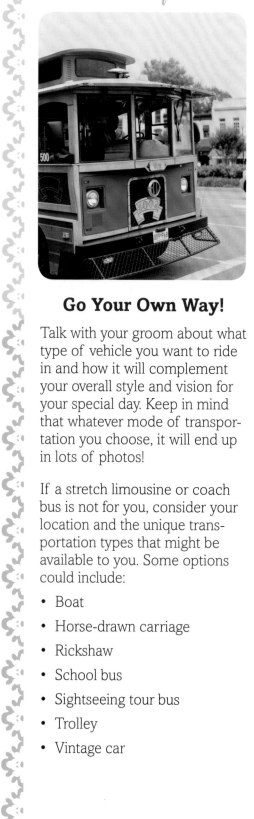

Go Your Own Way!

Talk with your groom about what type of vehicle you want to ride in and how it will complement your overall style and vision for your special day. Keep in mind that whatever mode of transportation you choose, it will end up in lots of photos!

If a stretch limousine or coach bus is not for you, consider your location and the unique transportation types that might be available to you. Some options could include:

- Boat
- Horse-drawn carriage
- Rickshaw
- School bus
- Sightseeing tour bus
- Trolley
- Vintage car

Consider Special Transportation for You and Your Groom

You and your groom will undoubtedly be excited and experience some wedding day nerves, so plan to have someone else chauffeur the two of you around on your special day. Write down a detailed schedule for you both, starting where you are first thing in the morning and all the places you will be going throughout the day and evening until you reach your overnight destination. Then plan how you will get from one place to the next.

Here are some prompts to help you make your schedule.

- Will your hair and makeup team be coming to you, or will you be going to them?

- Where will you be getting dressed, and how will you get there?

- Where will you be right before the ceremony and how will you get to the ceremony venue (if you aren't getting dressed there)—will you ride with your bridal party or parents?

- If you aren't getting dressed at your ceremony venue, is there a private space where you can wait until it is time for you to walk down the aisle, or will you have to wait in a vehicle?

- If your reception is not at the same venue as your ceremony, do you and your groom want to have a few moments alone during the ride to your reception venue?

- If you will be riding to your reception venue, are you planning to stop along the way to take photos?

- What is your "getaway" plan for leaving your wedding reception? Will you be going straight to a hotel for the evening or continuing the celebration at an after-reception party? How will you get from one place to another?

Arranging Transportation for Your Bridal Party

Providing transportation for the members of your bridal party will help ensure that the group stays together and arrives on time at your ceremony and reception venues. When you are arranging transportation for your bridesmaids, think about vehicles that will be easy for them to get into, out of, and sit in without wrinkling their attire. A small shuttle bus or a limousine might provide the perfect option for a fun, easy trip, with a celebratory glass of bubbly on the way to the reception venue after your ceremony.

Arranging Transportation for Your Guests

Depending on what your budget will allow, consider how many guests you can provide transportation for and what kind. Can you shuttle everyone in a bus to a remote location that has difficult driving terrain? Can you provide transportation only for out-of-town guests staying in blocks of rooms at a hotel, motel, or bed-and-breakfast? If most of your guests will be driving to your ceremony and/or reception venues, will there be enough suitable parking for all of the cars—or do you need to arrange a shuttle from a central parking area? If you are offering alcoholic beverages at your reception, would it be wise to provide a shuttle as a safe way for your guests to get to and from the venue?

If you have made transportation arrangements, post detailed information on your wedding Web site and also provide it on a wedding invitation insert so guests can plan accordingly. If you are providing transportation to your reception venue, plan to start shuttle service before the end of your ceremony—many elderly guests or guests with small children may not be able to comfortably stay through the entire ceremony, and they will appreciate the option of being able to leave earlier, if necessary.

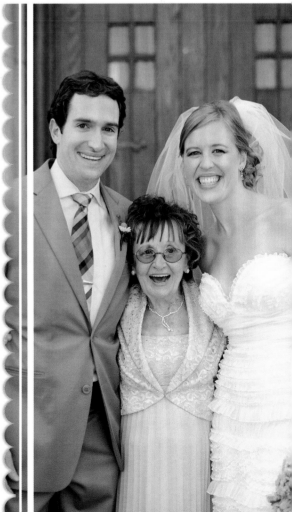

Providing Valet Parking Service

If your ceremony and reception venues do not have convenient, suitable parking, consider providing valet service. Some venues offer a valet parking service option, but others do not, and you will be responsible for booking it. Before you book a service, talk with the valet service representative about how many cars you anticipate will have to be parked and make sure there will be enough attendants who will be well prepared to meet your guests' needs.

details, details, details

Since most of your guests will use the restrooms during your reception, place small signs with the transportation schedule or taxicab phone numbers by the sinks or another spot where people will easily see them.

Enjoying Parties in Your Honor

Like other wedding-related events, engagement parties and bridal showers vary widely in size and complexity, and the themes and decorations can be customized to reflect the personalities and preferences of the bride and groom. Consider sharing your Buzz Words (page 14) and Inspiration Board (page 32) with the people who will be hosting parties in your honor so they know the overall look you want for your wedding celebration. If you have more ideas for your wedding ceremony or reception than your budget or final color and style choices allow, you could suggest using them as party themes and/or decorations.

Engagement Parties

Traditional etiquette suggests that only guests who will receive a wedding invitation should be invited to an engagement party to honor the bride and groom—but today people are hosting engagement parties for various groups of people who know the bride and/or groom from school, work, church, or other setting, regardless of whether they will be invited to the wedding. If the bride and groom come from different states or regions of the country, it makes sense to have several engagement parties—and bridal showers—in convenient locations for guests who want to be part of the wedding celebration but will be unable to travel to the ceremony or reception.

Bridal Showers

Usually hosted by the maid or matron of honor, a bridal shower traditionally includes the bride's female friends and family members, and the guests gift the bride with personal items, as well as items to furnish her home. In addition to the gift opening, a shower often includes enjoying favorite foods and beverages and playing simple wedding-related games. You may be honored at a bridal shower any time between the day you announce your engagement to shortly before your wedding.

Here are some tips to keep in mind.

- Whoever is hosting a party in your honor will direct guests to your gift registries for ideas. Be sure to complete your registries as soon after your engagement as you can, and include enough items at a variety of prices so guests will have a number of gift choices. If you know a planned party or shower has a theme, be sure to register for extra items that fit the theme. For a kitchen shower, for example, select extra utensils, place settings, and kitchen gadgets.

- Be a gracious guest of honor. Dress for the occasion, and arrive early. Be sure to talk with everyone at the party, and thank them for joining you.

- Ask your maid or matron of honor or one of your bridesmaids to keep a list of each gift and who gave it. This will make sending thank-you notes to the correct person a breeze.

- Graciously thank each gift giver. Even though you have registered your gift choices, some guests may prefer to give you something different. Be sure to acknowledge how much you enjoy each gift, even if it is not something you preselected.

- Bring a small thank-you gift for the person or people who planned and hosted the party. This could be a special bottle of wine, flowers, or a fragrant candle accompanied by a personal handwritten note.

- Send handwritten thank-you notes within two weeks of the shower. Personalize each note as much as possible to let each person know that you really appreciate her thoughtfulness.

Bachelor and Bachelorette Parties

The oftentimes long-awaited bachelor and bachelorette parties, traditionally planned by the best man and maid or matron of honor, mark the end of the groom's and bride's "single" status. Usually the members of the bridal party gather privately to relax and enjoy some carefree activity. Since these gatherings can sometimes lead to overindulgence in alcoholic beverages, try to plan them for a week—or even a month or two—before your wedding. It is not a good idea to head to the altar after a late night out, and you will appreciate a break from last-minute planning—and maybe even enjoy the parties more—if you don't have to worry about spoiling your special day.

make it yours

If the traditional night on the town doesn't fit your personality, consider some of the many other fun options to spend time with your attendants—perhaps a spa weekend, hiking trip, wine tasting, golf outing, or cooking class.

Rehearsal Dinner

The wedding party typically does a run-through of the entire ceremony the evening before the wedding. This ensures that everyone knows their parts and feels comfortable on the big day. Following the rehearsal, there's a rehearsal dinner so everyone can relax and celebrate before the wedding day. The event can be as intimate as the bride, groom, immediate families, and wedding party, or as large as including out-of-town guests and other close friends. Typically the groom and his family host the event.

The rehearsal dinner can be as formal or as casual as the couple wishes, but it should not upstage the big day. It can be a buffet-style dinner or a sit-down dinner, but, either way, assigning seats makes it easier to group guests together and let them get to know each other. The atmosphere should be such that toasting can be encouraged. The groom's father gets things started with a toast to the bride and her family. This can be followed by the best man, groomsmen, maid-of-honor, bridesmaids, and other friends. The toasts can be serious or may include a funny story about the bride or groom. It might also be the opportunity for the groom to pass out his groom's gifts.

The groom's family will select the menu ahead of time, making sure not to include dishes that will be served at the wedding. They may want to create place cards for the table. They might also decide to work with the bride's florist to create centerpieces that can then be used for the wedding reception.

Making Your Wish List and Completing Your Gift Registries

Gift registries allow you and your groom to preselect items you need and will use in your home. Traditionally, registries served to encourage guests to gift a couple with their preferred items, which can include everything from fine china teacups to televisions. Also consider completing a honeymoon registry, which allows guests to gift you with a dinner out, a massage, or an excursion you can enjoy on your honeymoon.

Before you head to your first store to set up a gift registry, make a wish list of items you need for your home. If you and your groom are combining his and your household belongings and will be sharing an apartment or house for the first time, chances are you already have multiples of certain items; decide which of your current belongings you want to keep, which ones you want to be replaced by a gift, and what you don't yet have. If you and your groom are already living together, you may have most of the items you need or want; look for any items that are showing wear and tear and consider replacing them with upgraded gift items.

Plan to register at more than one store and for a variety of items with a range of prices so people will have a choice of gifts. Try to start registering your gift selections before the first engagement party or bridal shower in your honor and complete the process no later than six months before your wedding. Here are a few tips on what to expect to help make registering enjoyable as well as efficient.

■ **Decide where you want to register.** For your guests' convenience, register at several stores such as a specialty shop for linens or china, one or two large, fine department or home stores for the bulk of your household items, and perhaps an electronics store and a sporting goods store for other items.

■ **Allow plenty of time for your first round.** Yes, you probably will need a few rounds of registering before you have completed comprehensive lists at each store. Be patient, and start the process the morning of a day when you and your groom have plenty of time. Take a break for lunch, and continue at your own pace.

■ **Meet with a registry representative at each store.** Most stores have a registry department and program so head there first and spend a little time with a store representative. Most stores offer free instruction on suggested items to register for, how many of each item, and price points to consider. If the registry representative does not offer a tour of the store, ask for one and any store-specific strategies on where to start selecting specific items.

■ **For your guests' convenience, ask for your registry to be available both at store location(s) and online.**

■ **Avoid the initial enticement of registering online before looking at the items in the store.** Compare options and jot down notes about specific items you prefer.

■ **When you think you have included all of the items you want, take a few minutes to edit the list.** Have you forgotten any items? Have you listed too many or two few choices?

■ **Register for extra pieces of specialty items such as fine china place settings, crystal and everyday glassware, and flatware.** Keep the extras in their original boxes so you won't have to search for a replacement in case one of your pieces chips or breaks in the years to come.

Avoid registering for seasonal items. If your wedding will be in the winter and you register during the previous summer, ask the store's registry representative if any of the items you have selected will be discounted or discontinued at the end of the season.

Confirm the address where your gifts will be delivered. If you are planning to move after your wedding, remember to update the "ship to" address on your registry so gifts that arrive after your wedding will reach you without any problem.

Ask about return policies. If your needs or wants change or you receive too many of one item, make sure you can return items for at least a store credit.

Post the Web site link to each store registry on your wedding Web page, or share it with a family member who will spread the word.

Maintain your registries. Check in regularly to see which of your preselected items have been purchased and if you need to add items to ensure your registry still includes a variety of items and prices.

Have thank-you notes ready to go. If you didn't order personalized thank-you note cards when you ordered your wedding stationery, be sure to order some when you start registering for gifts. Send a thank-you note within two weeks after receiving a gift. To help you remember who gave you each item, print a list of your registry from each store's Web site, and write the guest's name and the date you received each item.

Items to consider including on your gift registries

Notes:_____

_____

_____

_____

Dining Items
- [ ] Casual place settings
- [ ] Casual flatware
- [ ] Casual glassware
- [ ] Barware (specialty glasses, bar tools)
- [ ] Ice bucket
- [ ] Decanter
- [ ] Water pitcher
- [ ] Serving platters and bowls
- [ ] Serving utensils
- [ ] Table linens

Fine China, Crystal, and Silver
- [ ] Fine china place settings
- [ ] Coordinating china serving pieces
- [ ] Sterling silver flatware
- [ ] Crystal glassware
- [ ] Protective covers/storage pieces

Food Prep/Cooking Items
- [ ] Pots and pans
- [ ] Cooking and food prep utensils
- [ ] Knife block and specialty knives
- [ ] Cutting boards
- [ ] Stand and hand mixers
- [ ] Food processor
- [ ] Blender
- [ ] Juicer
- [ ] Toaster
- [ ] Toaster oven
- [ ] Baking sheets and cooling racks

- [ ] Oven mitts and potholders
- [ ] Dish drying rack
- [ ] Trash can and recycling bin

Bed and Bath
- [ ] Sheets sets
- [ ] Duvet cover
- [ ] Comforter
- [ ] Bed pillows
- [ ] Towels
- [ ] Shower curtain
- [ ] Bath accessories
- [ ] Hamper
- [ ] Scale

Decoration
- [ ] Toss pillows
- [ ] Vases
- [ ] Candleholders
- [ ] Coffee table books
- [ ] Picture frames and wall art
- [ ] Lamps
- [ ] Small storage pieces

Travel and Miscellaneous
- [ ] Carry-on and full-size luggage
- [ ] Vacuum cleaner
- [ ] Clothes drying rack
- [ ] Tool kit
- [ ] Car detail kit

Saying Thank-you with Personalized Gifts

Choosing Gifts for Your Bridesmaids

A nice way to thank your attendants for their personal support of you on your special day is to honor them with a bridal luncheon, which traditionally is hosted by the bride and her mother on or close to the wedding day. Your bridal luncheon can be as informal or formal as you prefer, and it doesn't have to be a luncheon at all—hosting a breakfast get-together on your wedding day or a group spa afternoon the day before offers perfect options for this special "no boys allowed" event.

Consider using this special time together to present your attendants with a small token of your appreciation. Regardless of what kind of gift you select, personalize it for each recipient. A piece of jewelry with an engraved personal sentiment or a gift certificate to each person's favorite hometown salon are two simple ideas to customize gifts. Here are a few other thoughtful gift ideas.

- A monogrammed bathrobe, pajamas, or cashmere cardigan
- A clutch and matching pashmina
- A personalized tote bag filled with each person's favorite beauty products
- The bridesmaids' dresses or special shoes
- A charm bracelet or other jewelry to wear on your wedding day
- Personalized correspondence cards
- Hair and makeup services on your wedding day
- A gift certificate to each person's favorite spa or specialty store
- A picture frame holding a special photo of you and the person

Choosing Gifts for Your Groomsmen

Encourage your groom to honor his attendants with a special wedding-related activity such as a golf outing or a hosted breakfast on your wedding day. Also consider giving each of the groomsmen a small gift from both of you to let them know how much you appreciate their support at this special time. Here are a few suggestions for groomsmen gifts.

- A personalized money clip, wallet, business card holder, or pen
- Cuff links personalized with each person's monogram or in the shape of an item related to something he enjoys
- The groomsmen's wedding day dress shirts and ties
- A pair of casual shoes
- Golf club covers
- Tickets to a sporting event
- A top-shelf bottle of each person's favorite liquor
- A subscription to a beer- or wine-of-the-month club
- A gift certificate to each person's favorite restaurant or specialty store

Thanking Your Parents

Your groom's parents and yours probably have played key roles in planning and paying for your wedding day, as well as personally supporting the two of you. While a simple thank you may be more than enough (a child's joy is one of the greatest gifts a parent can receive), consider giving them a handwritten note or card from the two of you, along with a special gift just for them. Here are a few gift suggestions that are sure to make Mom and Dad smile.

- A picture of your family in a personalized frame
- A bottle of fine Champagne for them to enjoy in their hotel room or at home after the wedding
- A gift certificate for dinner at their favorite restaurant
- An overnight stay at their favorite drivable destination

Planning Your Honeymoon

words of wisdom: Your honeymoon should be a time for the two of you to relax and unwind. If your schedules or budget do not allow for your dream vacation, consider taking a mini-moon for a few days after your wedding at a drivable destination. This will give you a little break from the wedding festivities and allow you to take your dream trip later at a more convenient time.

After the seemingly endless months of planning and the joyful excitement and busyness of your wedding day, your honeymoon will give you and your husband a chance to relax, unwind, and enjoy some much-deserved alone time basking in your post-wedding glow. Traditionally the groom or groom's family plans and pays for the honeymoon, but be sure to discuss your wants and needs as a couple before anyone makes any formal plans. To get the conversation started, consider the following.

- **Determine your budget.**

- **Brainstorm the type of honeymoon the two of you would enjoy together.** Everyone relaxes in different ways—you might opt for a weeklong trip on a secluded beachfront resort, or you might decide that a destination with plenty to do and see would be a better fit.

- **Consider how long you are willing to spend traveling to your destination.** Do you want a direct flight from your local airport—or do you mind having multiple layovers or even a couple of days of travel?

- **Decide when you want to travel.** Do you want to leave immediately after your reception, or do you want to spend a few days getting settled before you leave on a trip? Depending on your dream vacation location, you may choose to postpone your trip and wait for a more desirable season or affordable price.

- **If you are planning to travel internationally, consider enlisting the help of a travel agent.** These professionals know the ins and outs of the best locations to satisfy your wishes.

- **To get the best travel deals and flexible dates, plan ahead and book your final arrangements through a reputable source.**

- **If you are traveling out of the country, ask your doctor if you need any immunizations.** Be sure to leave plenty of time to schedule these.

Packing for Your Honeymoon

Use these tips on packing for your honeymoon.

- **Pack your suitcase(s) before your wedding day.** All you should need to add are toiletry items—place them in your luggage as soon as you finish using them on your wedding day.

- **Pack a separate suitcase for your wedding-related events.** If you are planning to check into a hotel for your wedding weekend, pack the items you need for the ceremony, reception, and any other events in a separate suitcase or garment bag. This will be especially handy if you are departing for your honeymoon immediately after your reception—all you have to do is hand off this suitcase or bag to the person who will take care of your wedding items while you are away.

- **Keep a change of clothes, basic TSA-size toiletries, and any valuables in your carry-on luggage.** If you arrive at your destination before the rest of your luggage, you will be set for at least a day.

- **Instead of packing separate his and her suitcases, consider dividing your clothing and shoes and sharing space in both suitcases.** This ensures that both of you will have something to wear if one of your suitcases gets lost.

- **Remember to pack sunscreen and any medications.**

- **Pack a few gallon-size resealable bags to accommodate things like wet bathing suits or sandy shoes on the trip home.** Include one or two additional quart-size bags—they will come in handy for carry-on toiletries if you misplace the ones you used earlier.

details, details, details

Bring a small bottle of lingerie wash or gentle hand-washing detergent with you. It will come in handy for keeping bathing suits and other items clean.

With decisions on the checklist complete and organized plans in place, the anticipation of your upcoming big day should be paired with both excitement and confidence.

As you close this chapter, the last "to do" on your checklist? Starting the next chapter of your life full of moments and memories that await you…at the end of the aisle.

{wed} v. To join in marriage.

Resources

Attire
Hitched | hitchedsalon.com
202.333.6162 | Washington, DC
pg. 51, 63

Cake
Just Cakes | justcakes.com
301.718.5111 | Bethesda, MD
pg. 196
Kendall's Cakes
kendallscakes.com | Washington, DC
703.536.2200 | pg. 194
Maggie Austin Cake
maggieaustincake.com
202.448.2920 | Washington, DC
pg. 194

Catering
Design Cuisine | designcuisine.com
703.979.9400 | Washington, DC
pg. 165, 194, 201, 206, 207, 214,
215, 216, 225, 231

Flowers
Amaryllis Inc.
amaryllisdesigns.com | 202.529.2230
Washington, DC | pg. 106, 170, 172,
182, 184, 186, 187, 188
Branch Design Studio
branchdesignstudio.com
843.847.7996 | Charleston, SC
pg. 180
Flower Follies | flowerfollies.com
410.212.9689 | Annapolis, MD
pg. 183
Flowers by Sidra Forman
sidraforman.com | 202.234.4598
Washington, DC | pg. 136, 137, 173,
175, 176, 178, 185, 188, 226
Franklin 215 Floral Design
jenniferlodato.com | 240.350.4754
Washington, DC | pg. 176

Helen Olivia Flowers
helenolivia.com | 703.548.2848
Alexandria, VA | pg. 246
**Holly Heider Chapple Flowers
Ltd.** | hollychappleflowers.com
703.777.8227 | Leesburg, VA
pg. 4, 110, 180, 183, 186, 188
LynnVale Studios | lynnvale.com
Gainesville, VA | pg. 186, 187
Philippa Tarrant Floral Design
philippatarrant.com | 202.413.8562
Washington, DC | pg. 169
Volanni | volanni.com
202.547.1603 | Washington, DC
pg. 181

Music
Carte Blanche
carteblanchesamples.com
888.800.3526 | New York, NY
pg. 234
Classical Guitar Ceremonies
chrisdunnguitar.com | 888.961.4048
Washington, DC | pg. 102
DJ D-Mac | djdmac.com
202.328.1967 | Washington, DC
pg. 238
Elan Artists | elanartists.com
888.800.3526 | New York, NY
pg. 234, 237
The Crystal Strings
sterling-artists.com | 301.262.3322
Washington, DC | pg. 232

Stationery & Calligraphy
Laura Hooper Calligraphy
lhcalligraphy.com | 818.259.7605
Los Angeles, CA | pg. 165, 219
Minted | minted.com | online only
pg. 148
Paper Moss | papermoss.com
800.511.0210 | Boston, MA | pg. 165

Rifle Paper Co. | rifledesign.com
Winter Park, FL | pg. 141, 166
SIMPLESONG Design
simplesongdesign.com
Washington, DC | pg. 142, 144, 148,
157, 161, 192, 195, 205, 214, 250,
257, 272

Tent
Skyline Tent Company
skylinetentcompany.com
434.977.8368 | Charlottesville, VA
pg. 199, 272

Wedding Planners
Ritzy Bee Events | ritzybee.com
703.508.7132 | Washington, DC
pg. 16, 114, 136, 137, 170, 172, 184,
185, 188, 186, 192, 194, 195, 199,
201, 202, 205, 219, 226, 232, 246,
248, 250, 257, 264, 271, 272
**Alexandra & Company
Events** | alexandracompany.com
202.330.3937 | Washington, DC
pg. 162, 215
Simply Chic Events
asimplychicevent.com
703.220.1287 | Washington, DC
pg. 227, 185, 187
**Atrendy Wedding & Event
Company** | atrendywedding.com
703.932.2185 | Washington, DC
pg. 98, 273
The Dazzling Details
thedazzlingdetails.com | Mexico
pg. 18, 37, 116, 221
Pineapple Productions
pineapplepro.com | Washington, DC
202.243.3160 | pg. 261

Index

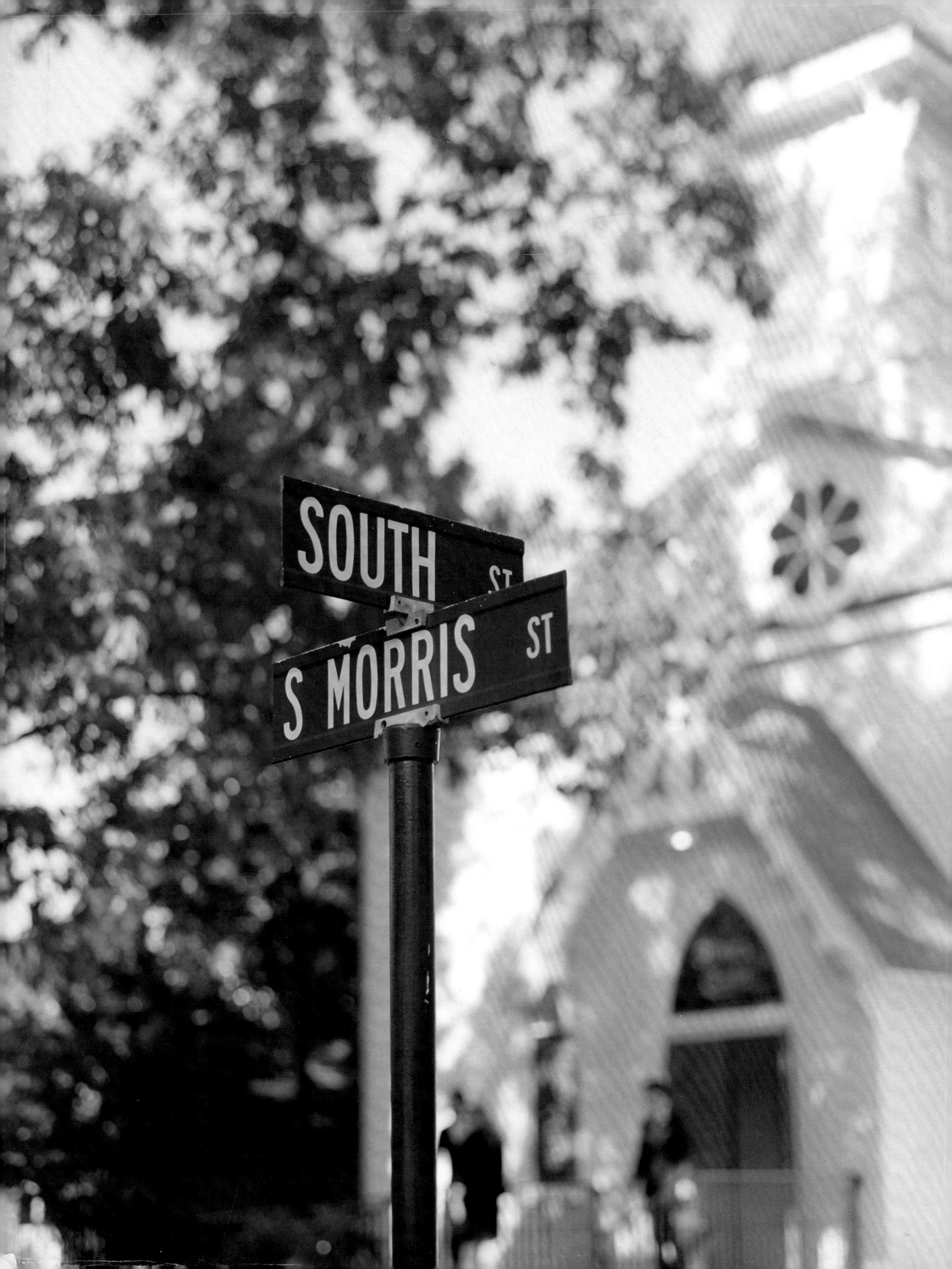
SOUTH ST
S MORRIS ST